Name:

CN00806941

Essential Exam Practice

Key Stage 4 Mathematics
Intermediate Level

Ruso Bradley and June Hall

Introduction

We believe mathematics is a subject where practice is the key to exam success. There can be no better way of boosting your grade than practising the type of questions that will come up in your exams. It is no secret that many questions come up year after year, which is why the Essential Exam Practice range concentrates on these extremely important questions. It is also true that you can't predict exactly what will be in your exams, but we think that we have pretty much covered all the options!

About this book

This book is aimed at candidates taking the Intermediate tier in GCSE Mathematics, and is suitable for all examination boards.

The questions are split into four main sections:
● Number (N)
● Algebra (A)
● Shape, Space & Measures (S)
● Handling Data (H)

Within these sections, the questions are grouped by topic, so you can quickly find what you're looking for. Answers to all questions can be found at the back of the book, so you can check that you're on the right track.

Good luck in your exams!

Contents

Number

N1 A landscape gardener bought 486 garden shrubs, at 62p each, from a local garden centre.

   (a) Without using a calculator and showing all your working, work out how much the landscape gardener spent on the shrubs.

Answer £ .... *(2 marks)*

The garden centre gives its customers an extra shrub free for every 18 bought.

   (b) How many extra shrubs did the landscape gardener get?
   Show all your working.

Answer .... *(2 marks)*

N2 DO NOT use a calculator for this question. Show all your working.

There were 713 runners in a half-marathon race. Each competitor had to pay 74p towards the cost of the first aid tent.

   (a) How much, in total, did the runners contribute towards the first aid tent?

Answer £ .... *(2 marks)*

NON-CALCULATOR MULTIPLICATION & DIVISION

The organisers of the race were obliged to hire 1 safety marshal for every 23 runners.

(b) How many safety marshals did they have to hire?

Answer .... *(2 marks)*

MULTIPLES & FACTORS

N3 Look at the list of numbers below.

1, 3, 9, 12, 16

(a) From the list, write down all the multiples of 3.

Answer ....*(1 mark)*

(b) Write down all the numbers in the list that are factors of 12.

Answer ....*(1 mark)*

m and n are two different numbers from the list.
m is a factor of 12 and $m = 4n$.

(c) Find m and n.

....

....

Answer $m =$ ....

$n =$ .... *(2 marks)*

Number

MULTIPLES & FACTORS

N4 From the list of numbers 2, 4, 6, 9, 10, 11, write down

    (a)   all the multiples of 2

        Answer ....*(1 mark)*

    (b)   all the factors of 10.

        Answer ....*(1 mark)*

x and y are two different numbers from the list.
x is a factor of 10 and y is a multiple of 3.

$$x = \frac{5}{3}y$$

    (c)   Find x and y.

    ....

    ....

        Answer $x = $ .... $y = $ .... *(2 marks)*

LCM & HCF

N5 Find the least common multiple of each set of numbers.

    (a)   6, 15

    ....

        Answer ....*(1 mark)*

    (b)   12, 21, 42

    ....

    ....

        Answer .... *(2 marks)*

N6 Find the least common multiple of each set of numbers.

    (a)   4, 6

....

Answer ....*(1 mark)*

    (b)   12, 16, 24

....

....

Answer .... *(2 marks)*

N7 Find the highest common factor of each set of numbers.

    (a)   5, 7

....

Answer ....*(1 mark)*

    (b)   12, 16, 24

....

....

Answer .... *(2 marks)*

N8 Find the highest common factor of each set of numbers.

    (a)   26, 39

....

Answer ....*(1 mark)*

    (b)   12, 36, 42

....

....

Answer .... *(2 marks)*

Number

LCM & HCF

N9 Calculate the shortest length of rope that can be cut into an exact number of 4 m lengths, 7 m lengths or 14 m lengths.

....

....

Answer .... m *(2 marks)*

N10 Calculate the shortest length of string that can be cut into an exact number of 3 cm lengths, 6 cm lengths or 8 cm lengths.

....

....

Answer ....cm *(2 marks)*

FRACTIONS & DECIMALS

N11 Arrange this set of fractions in order of size, smallest first.

$$\frac{2}{3} \qquad \frac{1}{4} \qquad \frac{3}{7} \qquad \frac{2}{5}$$

....

....

Answer .... *(2 marks)*

N12 Arrange this set of fractions in order of size, largest first.

$$\frac{1}{3} \qquad \frac{1}{2} \qquad \frac{2}{7} \qquad \frac{5}{11}$$

....

....

Answer .... *(2 marks)*

N13 A golf club has 360 members, 24 of which are junior members. What fraction of members are juniors? Reduce your answer to its lowest terms.

....

Answer .... *(2 marks)*

N14 During November it snowed on 5 days. On what fraction of days in November did snow fall? Reduce your answer to its lowest terms.

....

Answer .... *(2 marks)*

N15 Find as a fraction in its lowest terms:

(a) $\frac{1}{7} + \frac{2}{35}$

....

Answer .... *(2 marks)*

(b) $\frac{4}{5} - \frac{1}{2}$

....

Answer .... *(2 marks)*

(c) $\frac{2}{10} \div \frac{1}{5}$

....

Answer .... *(2 marks)*

N16 Find as a fraction in its lowest terms:

(a) $\frac{1}{20} + \frac{3}{4}$

....

Answer .... *(2 marks)*

(b) $\frac{7}{8} - \frac{1}{4}$

....

Answer .... *(2 marks)*

(c) $\frac{3}{11} \times \frac{22}{45}$

....

Answer .... *(2 marks)*

N17 A bag holds 1 kg of salt. What fraction of its weight remains after 200 g of salt is used?

....

Answer .... *(2 marks)*

N18 Tony received £10 for his birthday, a quarter of which he spent on a CD. He spent a third of the remaining money on a magazine. How much money did Tony have left?

....

....

Answer £ .... *(3 marks)*

N19 (a) Change 0.2 into a fraction in its lowest terms.

....

Answer .... *(2 marks)*

(b) Write down the value of 0.2×100.

Answer .... *(1 mark)*

(c) Write down the value of $0.2 \div 100$.

Answer .... *(1 mark)*

N20 **(a)** Convert 0.15 into a fraction in its lowest terms.

....

Answer .... *(2 marks)*

(b) Write down the value of 0.15×100.

Answer .... *(1 mark)*

(c) Write down the value of $0.15 \div 100$.

Answer .... *(1 mark)*

N21 A piece of elastic, 12.5 cm long, is cut into 50 pieces of equal length.
How long is each piece?

....

Answer .... cm *(1 mark)*

N22 If 16.5 kg of butter is divided between 33 people, how much butter does each person get?

....

Answer .... kg *(1 mark)*

N23 A wooden box full of coffee beans weighs 40 kg.
The coffee beans on their own weigh 35 kg.

(a) What percentage of the total weight is the weight of the coffee beans?

....

Answer .... % *(2 marks)*

(b) What percentage of the total weight is the weight of the wooden box?

....

Answer .... % *(1 mark)*

Number

N24 Out of 32 teams in a basketball tournament, 20 of them play in red shorts.

   (a) What percentage of teams play in red shorts?

      ....

                Answer .... % *(2 marks)*

   (b) What percentage of teams do not play in red shorts?

      ....

                Answer .... % *(1 mark)*

N25 Jemba and Beth share £39 in the ratio 5:8.

   (a) What is Jemba's share?

      ....

      ....

                Answer £ .... *(2 marks)*

   (b) What percentage of the money is Beth's?

      ....

      ....

                Answer .... % *(2 marks)*

N26 Anthony and Sarah share £55 in the ratio 4:7.

   (a) What is Sarah's share?

      ....

      ....

                Answer £ .... *(2 marks)*

(b) What percentage of the money belongs to Anthony?

....

....

Answer .... % *(2 marks)*

N27 At a timber merchants, pine costs £20 per cubic foot.
Oak costs 15% more per cubic foot than pine.

(a) How much, per cubic foot, does oak cost?

....

....

Answer £ .... *(2 marks)*

Mahogany costs 25% more than oak.

(b) How much, per cubic foot, is mahogany?

....

....

Answer £ .... *(2 marks)*

N28 Red grapes cost £1.90 per kg. White grapes cost 20% more.
How much do white grapes cost?

....

....

Answer £ .... per kg *(2 marks)*

N29 Two kilograms of tuna costs £2.60.
How much will 5 kg cost?

....

....

Answer £ .... *(2 marks)*

Number

N30 4 pints of orange juice cost £3.20.
How much will 11 pints of orange juice cost?

....

....

Answer £ .... *(2 marks)*

N31 A chocolate cake for 5 people requires 75 g of sugar.
Daphne makes a chocolate cake for 8 people.

(a) Calculate the weight of sugar that Daphne needs.

....

Answer .... g *(2 marks)*

(b) Daphne cuts the cake into 8 equal slices. Her friends eat 5 slices of the cake. What percentage of the cake is left?

....

Answer .... % *(2 marks)*

N32 A pizza for 7 people requires 840 g of flour. Dennis makes a pizza for 4 people.

(a) Calculate the weight of flour that Dennis needs for his pizza.

....

Answer .... g *(2 marks)*

(b) Dennis eats 1 person's share of the pizza.
What percentage of the pizza is left?

....

Answer .... % *(2 marks)*

N33 A new car is on sale for £12 000. The car's value will decrease by 15% each year.

    (a) How much will the car be worth after 1 year?

        ....

                Answer £ .... *(2 marks)*

    (b) How much will the car be worth after 2 years?

        ....

                Answer £ ....*(2 marks)*

N34 Remi puts £5000 in a savings account that offers 5% interest per year.
Interest is added to the account at the end of each year.

How much money will be in Remi's account after 3 years if he doesn't make any further deposits or withdrawals?

        ....

        ....

                Answer £ ....*(3 marks)*

N35 A double glazing manufacturer reduced the price of their most expensive front door from £620 to £540. What was the percentage reduction in price?

        ....

                Answer .... % *(2 marks)*

N36 Shortly after 25 December, the price of tinsel dropped from £2.10 to £1.60.
What was the percentage reduction in price?

        ....

                Answer .... % *(2 marks)*

Number

PERCENTAGES, RATIO & PROPORTION

N37 A house rose in value by 15% to £72 000 over the last year.

(a) What was the value of the house a year ago?

....

Answer £ .... *(3 marks)*

The value of another house dropped by 5% to £68 000 over the same period.

(b) What was the value of this house a year ago?

....

Answer £ .... *(3 marks)*

N38 A bottle of vintage wine has risen in value by 10%, to £1200, over the last 5 years.

(a) How much was the bottle of wine worth 5 years ago?

....

Answer £ .... *(3 marks)*

In fact, at £1200 the wine is now worth 5% more than it was a year ago.

(b) How much was the wine worth a year ago?

....

Answer £ .... *(3 marks)*

POWERS & ROOTS

N39 **(a)** Work out the value of 0.046^2.

Answer ....*(1 mark)*

(b) Given that x is positive and $x^2 = 0.0529$, find the value of x.

....

Answer $x =$ ....*(1 mark)*

N40 Work out the value of these.

   (a) 2^6

....

Answer .... *(1 mark)*

   (b) 5^3

....

Answer .... *(1 mark)*

   (c) $8^{\frac{2}{3}}$

....

Answer .... *(2 marks)*

   (d) $10^2 \times 10^3$

....

Answer .... *(2 marks)*

   (e) $9^4 \div 9^2$

....

Answer .... *(2 marks)*

   (f) $\dfrac{4^8}{4^3 \times 4^2}$

....

....

Answer .... *(3 marks)*

N41 A square-shaped patio has an area of 12.25 m^2.
What is the length of one side of the patio?

....

Answer .... m *(1 mark)*

Number

N42   A cube shaped box of sugar has a volume of 274.625 cm³.
What is the length of one side of the box?

....

Answer .... cm *(1 mark)*

PRIMES & SPECIAL NUMBERS

N43   Below is a list of numbers.

$$7, 9, 10, 12, 16, 27$$

(a)   Which number is a cube number?

Answer .... *(1 mark)*

(b)   Which two numbers are square numbers?

Answer ....*(1 mark)*

(c)   Which number is a triangular number?

Answer ....*(1 mark)*

(d)   From the list, find two numbers x and y such that $\frac{x^2}{3} = y$.

....

....

Answer $x = $ ...., $y = $ .... *(2 marks)*

N44   Write down all the prime numbers that are

(a)   even

Answer ....*(1 mark)*

(b)   multiples of 3

Answer ....*(1 mark)*

(c)   between 20 and 30.

Answer .... *(2 marks)*

N45 x, y and z are different numbers in this list:

$$3, 7, 9, 12, 13, 15, 16$$

x is a triangular number.
y is a prime number.
z is a square number.
$x + y = z$

Work out the values of x, y and z.

....

....

....

Answer $x =$ ....

$y =$ ....

$z =$ .... *(2 marks)*

N46 a, b and c are different numbers in the list below.

$$3, 5, 8, 10, 11, 16, 19$$

a and b are prime numbers.
c is a cube number.
$a - b = c$.

Work out the values of a, b and c.

....

....

....

Answer $a =$ ....

$b =$ ....

$c =$ .... *(2 marks)*

Number

N47 The prime factorisation of a certain number is

$$2^2 \times 3^2 \times 7$$

(a) What is the number?

Answer ....(1 mark)

(b) Write down the prime factorisation of 90.

....

....

Answer .... (2 marks)

N48 (a) Write 275 as a product of its prime factors.

....

....

Answer .... (2 marks)

(b) The prime factorisation of 180 can be written in the form

$$2^x \times 3^y \times 5^z$$

Find x, y and z.

....

....

....

Answer $x = $...

$y = $...

$z = $... (2 marks)

N49 Convert the improper fraction $\frac{8}{7}$ to a decimal correct to:

    (a)   2 decimal places

              Answer ....*(1 mark)*

    (b)   2 significant figures

              Answer ....*(1 mark)*

N50 Convert the improper fraction $\frac{11}{9}$ to a decimal correct to:

    (a)   3 decimal places

              Answer ....*(1 mark)*

    (b)   3 significant figures

              Answer ....*(1 mark)*

N51 (a)   Find an approximate value of the expression

$$\frac{20.3 \times 51.2}{498.6}$$

        ....

              Answer .... *(2 marks)*

    (b)   The entire surface of a sphere of radius 5.2 m is to be painted.
           There is enough paint to cover 280 m^2.
           (Surface area of a sphere $= 4\pi r^2$)

           Use approximations to estimate whether there is enough paint to cover the sphere.

        ....

        .... *(3 marks)*

N52 (a)   Find an approximate value of the expression

$$\frac{409.2 \times 0.523}{41.6}$$

        ....

              Answer .... *(2 marks)*

Number

(b) The entire surface of the cube shown is to be painted. There is enough paint to cover 5000 cm².

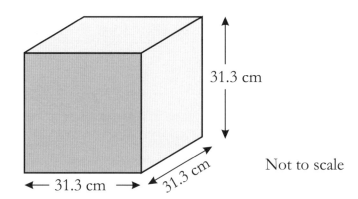

31.3 cm

← 31.3 cm →   31.3 cm

Not to scale

Use approximations to estimate whether there is enough paint.

....

.... *(3 marks)*

N53 Calculate, giving your answer to an appropriate degree of accuracy:

$$\frac{29.42 \times 0.0941}{15.2 \times 8.42}$$

....

Answer .... *(2 marks)*

N54 Calculate, giving your answer to an appropriate degree of accuracy:

$$\frac{9.59 \times 0.024}{7.2 \times 1.4}$$

....

Answer .... *(2 marks)*

NEGATIVE NUMBERS

N55 The diagram shows an aeroplane 126 m above the sea and a submarine below the surface.

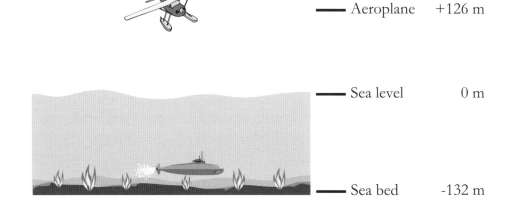

—— Aeroplane   +126 m

—— Sea level   0 m

—— Sea bed   -132 m

22

(a) How far is the sea bed below the aeroplane?

....

Answer .... m *(1 mark)*

The base of the submarine is 46 m above the sea bed.

(b) How far below sea level is the base of the submarine?

....

Answer .... m *(2 marks)*

N56 (a) According to the map, how much warmer is Portugal than Sweden?

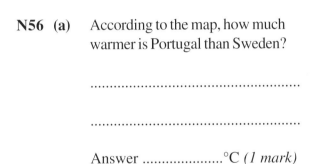

....

....

Answer ....°C *(1 mark)*

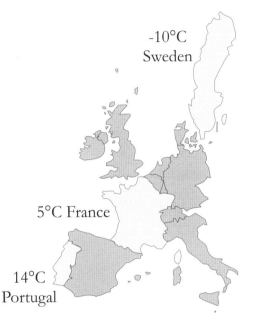

-10°C
Sweden

5°C France

14°C
Portugal

(b) The temperatures drop to 10°C below those shown on the map. What is the new temperature in:

Sweden .... °C

France .... °C *(2 marks)*

N57 Complete these calculations:

(a)   -6 + -4 = ...

(b)   -6 − -4 = ...

(c)   9 × -3 = ...

(d)   9 ÷ -3 = ...

(4 marks)

Number

N58 Complete these calculations:

(a) -3 + 5 = ...

(b) -3 – -5 = ...

(c) -12 × -3 = ...

(d) -12 ÷ -3 = ...   *(4 marks)*

STANDARD INDEX FORM

N59 (a) Write 920 000 in standard form.

Answer ....*(1 mark)*

(b) Write 4.3×10^5 as an ordinary number.

Answer ....*(1 mark)*

N60 (a) What is 0.0423 in standard form?

Answer .... *(1 mark)*

(b) What is 5.9×10^7 written as an ordinary number?

Answer ....*(1 mark)*

N61 The population of India is roughly 850 million.
India's surface area is approximately $3 \times 10^6 \, \text{km}^2$.

(a) Write the population of India in standard form.

Answer ....*(1 mark)*

(b) Giving your answer in standard form, calculate the approximate average area, in km², per head of population.

....

....

Answer .... km² *(2 marks)*

N62 The Moon is 384 000 km from the Earth's surface.
The diameter of the Moon is $3.5 \times 10^3 \, \text{km}$.

(a) Write the distance between the Moon and the Earth in standard form.

Answer .... km *(1 mark)*

(b) In terms of the diameter of the Moon, how far is the Moon from the Earth?

....

....

Answer .... Moon diameters *(2 marks)*

N63 An encyclopedia contains 6.2×10^2 pages, printed on both sides.

(a) The thickness of a page is 7.4×10^{-3} cm.
Disregarding the cover, what is the thickness of the encyclopedia?

....

Answer .... cm *(2 marks)*

(b) Without the cover, the encyclopedia weighs 4.2×10^2 g.
What is the weight of a single page?

....

....

Answer .... g *(2 marks)*

N64 The Arctic Ocean has a surface area of 1.4×10^7 km^2 and an average depth of 1.3×10^3 m. The Pacific Ocean has a surface area of 1.8×10^8 km^2 and an average depth of 4.3×10^3 m.

(a) In terms of surface area, how many times bigger is the Pacific Ocean than the Arctic Ocean?

....

....

Answer .... *(2 marks)*

(b) On average, how many times deeper is the Pacific Ocean than the Arctic Ocean?

....

....

Answer .... *(2 marks)*

Algebra

A1 Simplify the following:

(a) $4x + 5y - 3x + 6y$

....

Answer ....*(2 marks)*

(b) $a^2 \times a^4$

....

Answer ....*(2 marks)*

(c) $\dfrac{15x^6}{3x^4}$

....

Answer ....*(2 marks)*

A2 (a) Express $\dfrac{9x^3 \times 4x^3}{12x^2}$ as simply as possible.

....

Answer ....*(2 marks)*

(b) Combine as a single fraction: $\dfrac{x}{3} + \dfrac{x^2}{6}$

....

Answer ....*(2 marks)*

A3 Simplify:

(a) $\dfrac{x^3}{x} - \dfrac{x^2}{2}$

....

Answer ....*(2 marks)*

(b) $\dfrac{5x^4 \times 4x^3}{10x^5}$

....

Answer ....*(2 marks)*

Algebra

A4 Solve the equations:

(a) $5x = 2$

....

Answer $x =$ ....*(1 mark)*

(b) $15 - 3x = 3$

....

....

Answer $x =$ .... *(2 marks)*

(c) $16 - 2x = 4x + 10$

....

....

Answer $x =$ .... *(2 marks)*

(d) $4(2x - 1) = 7x + 11$

....

....

....

Answer $x =$ .... *(3 marks)*

(e) $\dfrac{180}{x + 3} = 12$

....

....

....

Answer $x =$ .... *(3 marks)*

Algebra

A5   Solve the following equations:

(a) $11y = 5$

....

Answer $y =$ .... *(1 mark)*

(b) $11 - 6y = -1$

....

....

Answer $y =$ .... *(2 marks)*

(c) $14 + 9y = 5y + 26$

....

....

Answer $y =$ .... *(2 marks)*

(d) $3(5y + 6) = 20y + 8$

....

....

....

Answer $y =$ .... *(3 marks)*

(e) $\dfrac{150}{y + 3} = 10$

....

....

....

Answer $y =$ .... *(3 marks)*

Algebra

A6   Peri bought 4 books and a bedside lamp from a jumble sale. The lamp cost £8 and he spent £32 in total.

   (a)   If each book cost £x, write down an equation in x.

Answer .... *(2 marks)*

   (b)   Solve your equation to find the cost of one book.

....

....

Answer £ .... *(2 marks)*

A7   Donald buys 4 jars of garlic paste and a pot of ground coriander from the supermarket. The pot of coriander weighs 12 g. The whole bag of shopping weighs 852 g.

   (a)   Write down an equation in y, where y represents the weight of one jar of garlic paste.

Answer .... *(2 marks)*

   (b)   Solve the equation for y and hence write down the weight of 1 jar of garlic paste.

....

....

Answer .... g *(2 marks)*

A8   If $x = 3$ and $y = 2.5$, what is the value of:

   (a) $2xy$

....

Answer .... *(2 marks)*

   (b) $3x^2 + 2y$

....

Answer .... *(2 marks)*

Algebra

SUBSTITUTING VALUES

A9 Given that $A = 3$ and $B = \frac{2}{3}$, work out the value of:

(a) $\dfrac{AB}{A^2}$

....

....

Answer .... *(2 marks)*

(b) $A(B + A)$

....

....

Answer .... *(2 marks)*

A10 The time needed to cook a turkey is given as 20 minutes per pound plus an extra 20 minutes.

(a) Write down a formula for the time taken, T, to cook a turkey of weight W lb.

Answer $T =$ .... *(2 marks)*

(b) How long will a turkey weighing 8 lb take to cook? Give your answer in hours.

....

Answer .... hours *(2 marks)*

A11 Salespeople are paid according to how many hours they work and the number of products they sell.

(a) If a salesperson receives £6 per hour plus £2 for every item sold, write down a formula for their pay, P, in terms of hours worked, H, and number of items sold, S.

Answer $P = £$ .... *(2 marks)*

(b) How much does a salesperson get paid for 7 hours work if 15 items are sold?

....

Answer £ .... *(2 marks)*

A12 Make a the subject of the formula $b = a^2 + 2$.

....

Answer $a =$... *(2 marks)*

A13 You are given the formula $a = 2bc^2$.

   (a) Rearrange the formula to give b in terms of a and c.

   ....

Answer $b =$... *(2 marks)*

   (b) Rearrange the formula to give c in terms of a and b.

   ....

   ....

Answer $c =$... *(2 marks)*

A14 $v^2 = u^2 + 2as$ is a formula used in physics.

   (a) Rearrange the formula to give a in terms of u, v and s.

   ....

   ....

Answer $a =$... *(2 marks)*

   (b) Rearrange the formula to give u in terms of v, a and s.

   ....

   ....

Answer $u =$... *(2 marks)*

Algebra

A15 **(a)** Draw the graph of $y = 3 - x$ for values of x between -3 and 3.

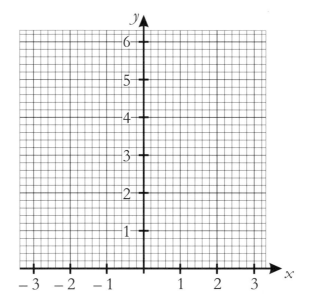

(3 marks)

(b) At what value does the graph cross the y-axis?

Answer $y =$ ....*(1 mark)*

(c) What is the gradient of the graph?

Answer ....*(1 mark)*

A16 **(a)** By first constructing and completing a table of values, draw the graph of $y = 3x - 2$ for values of x from 0 to 6. *(3 marks)*

x							
y							

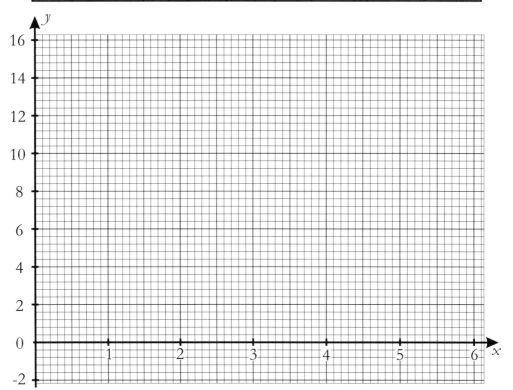

(b) At what value does the line cross the y-axis?

Answer $y =$ ....*(1 mark)*

(c) What is the gradient of the line?

Answer ....*(1 mark)*

A17 The cost of hiring a taxi includes a fixed amount and a charge per mile travelled, and is shown in the graph below.

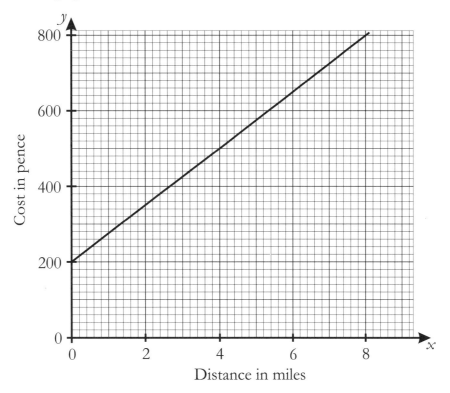

(a) Find the equation of the line in the form $y = ax + b$.

....

....

....

Answer $y =$ ....*(3 marks)*

(b) Calculate the cost of travelling 10 miles in the taxi.

....

....

Answer £ ....*(2 marks)*

Algebra

A18 The cost of hiring an emergency plumber includes a fixed call out charge and a charge per hour worked, and is shown in the graph below.

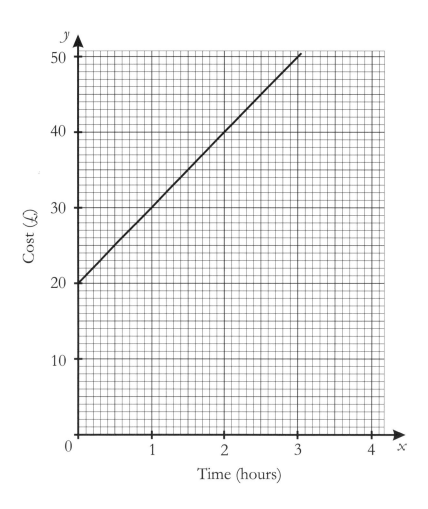

(a) Find the equation of the line in the form $y = ax + b$.

....

....

....

Answer $y =$ .... *(3 marks)*

(b) Calculate the cost of hiring the plumber for 5 hours.

....

....

Answer £ .... *(2 marks)*

Algebra

STRAIGHT LINES

A19 Which of these lines is parallel to the line with equation $2y = 4x - 6$?

$y = 3 - 2x$ $y = 4x - 3$ $y = 2x + 18$

....

....

Answer .... *(2 marks)*

SIMULTANEOUS EQUATIONS

A20 Solve algebraically the simultaneous equations below.

$$4x + 7y = 10$$
$$2x + 3y = 3$$

....

....

....

....

Answer $x = $ ...., $y = $ .... *(3 marks)*

A21 Solve algebraically:

$$9x + 11y = 15$$
$$4x + 4y = 4$$

....

....

....

....

Answer $x = $ ...., $y = $ .... *(3 marks)*

35

Algebra

SIMULTANEOUS EQUATIONS

A22 On the axes below, draw graphs of:

(a) $y = 2x + 2$

(b) $y = 10 - 2x$

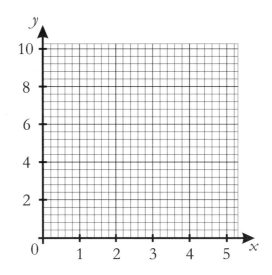

(3 marks)

(c) Write down the value of x where the graphs meet.

Answer $x =$ ....*(1 mark)*

A23 On the graph paper below, draw the graphs of:

(a) $y = 2x$

(b) $y = 6 - x$

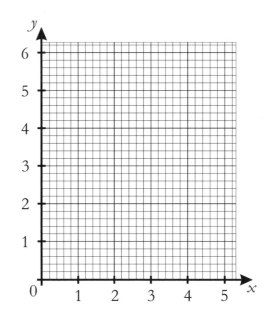

(3 marks)

(c) Write down the value of y where the graphs meet.

Answer $y =$ ....*(1 mark)*

A24 List all the possible values of x such that $-5 \leqslant x < 4$, where x is an integer.

.... *(2 marks)*

A25 Write down all the values of x that satisfy $-2 < x \leqslant 6$, where x is an integer.

.... *(2 marks)*

A26 (a) Represent $x < 4$ on the number line below.

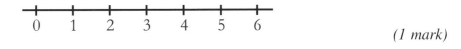

(1 mark)

(b) Represent $-1 < x \leqslant 3$ on the number line below.

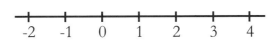

(2 marks)

A27 (a) Solve the inequality $3(4x + 3) < 15$.

....

....

....

Answer .... *(2 marks)*

(b) Shade the single region that satisfies $y > 1$, $y \geqslant x$ and $x < 3$.

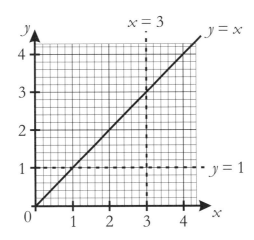

(1 mark)

Algebra

A28 **(a)** Solve the inequality $5(3x-7)<5$.

....

....

....

Answer .... *(2 marks)*

(b) Shade the region that satisfies $y \leqslant 5$, $y+2x>6$ and $y>x$.

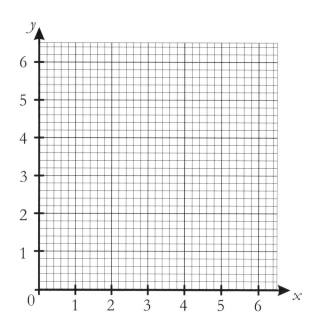

(4 marks)

A29 Showing all your trials, use trial and improvement to solve $x^2 = 7$.
(Give your answer correct to 1 decimal place.)

....

....

....

Answer $x = $ .... *(3 marks)*

Algebra

A30 Using trial and improvement, solve $x^3 = 11$.
(Give your answer correct to 1 decimal place.)

....

....

....

Answer $x =$ .... *(3 marks)*

A31 Using trial and improvement, solve $x^3 + x = 500$.
(Give your answer correct to 1 decimal place.)

....

....

....

Answer $x =$ .... *(3 marks)*

A32 (a) Multiply out the brackets and simplify the expression $(2x + 9)(x - 7)$.

....

Answer .... *(2 marks)*

(b) Multiply out the brackets and collect together like terms.

$$x(2x^2 + 3) + x^2(x + 2) + x(x + 3)$$

....

....

Answer .... *(2 marks)*

(c) Factorise $x^2 + 5x + 6$.

....

....

Answer .... *(2 marks)*

Algebra

EXPANSION & FACTORISATION

A33 **(a)** Simplify, by first multiplying out the brackets: $(3x-2)(5x+4)$

....

Answer .... *(2 marks)*

(b) Simplify the following expression: $x(x+2) + x^2(x+2) + x(x^2+1)$

....

....

Answer .... *(2 marks)*

(c) Factorise $x^2 + 2x - 8$.

....

....

Answer .... *(2 marks)*

QUADRATICS

A34 **(a)** Factorise $x^2 - 4x$.

....

Answer .... *(2 marks)*

(b) Solve $x^2 - 4x = 0$.

....

Answer $x =$ .... *(2 marks)*

A35 **(a)** Factorise $x^2 - 9$.

....

Answer .... *(2 marks)*

(b) Solve $x^2 - 9 = 0$.

....

Answer $x = $ .... *(2 marks)*

A36 Solve $x^2 - x - 12 = 0$.

....

....

Answer $x = $ .... *(3 marks)*

A37 Find both solutions to $x^2 - 3x - 10 = 0$.

....

....

Answer $x = $ .... *(3 marks)*

A38 These two rectangles have the same area:

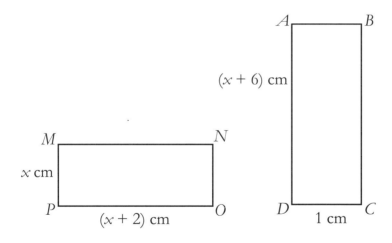

Not to scale

(a) Form an equation in x and show that it can be simplified to $x^2 + x - 6 = 0$.

....

....

.... *(2 marks)*

(b) Solve the equation $x^2 + x - 6 = 0$ to find the length of MP.

....

....

....

....

Answer $MP =$ .... cm *(4 marks)*

A39 The perimeter of a rectangle is 32 cm and its length is x cm.

(a) Find an expression for the width of the rectangle in terms of x.

....

....

Answer .... cm *(2 marks)*

(b) Using the fact that the area of the rectangle is 48 cm², form an equation involving x and show that it can be simplified to $x^2 - 16x + 48 = 0$.

....

.... *(2 marks)*

(c) Solve the equation $x^2 - 16x + 48 = 0$ to find the 2 possible lengths of the rectangle.

....

....

....

Answer .... cm *(4 marks)*

A40 A right-angled triangle has sides of length x cm, $(x-1)$ cm and $(x-8)$ cm.

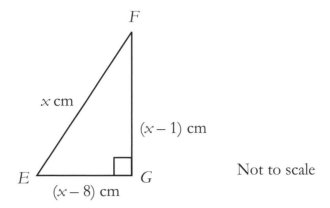

Not to scale

(a) Form an equation in x and show that it simplifies to $x^2 - 18x + 65 = 0$.

....

....

.... *(3 marks)*

(b) Solve the equation and hence find the length of the hypotenuse.

....

....

....

....

Answer .... cm *(4 marks)*

Algebra

A41 **(a)** By first completing the table, draw the graph of $y = 3x^2$ for values of x from 0 to 3.

x				
x^2				
$y = 3x^2$				

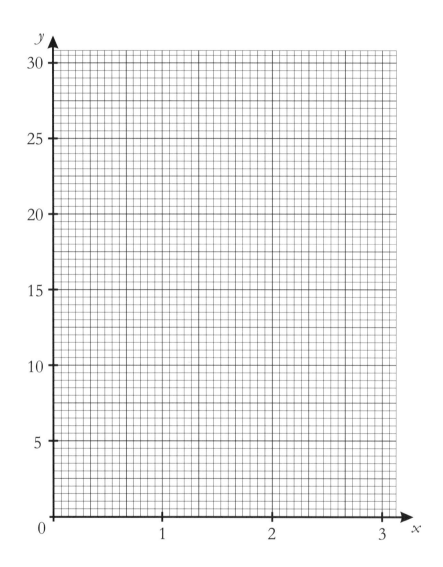

(3 marks)

(b) Use your graph to find a value of x when $y = 20$.

Answer $x =$ ....*(1 mark)*

44

A42 **(a)** Complete the table of values for $y = x^2 - 2x - 1$.

x	-3	-2	-1	0	1	2	3
y							

(b) Draw the graph of $y = x^2 - 2x - 1$ on the graph paper below.

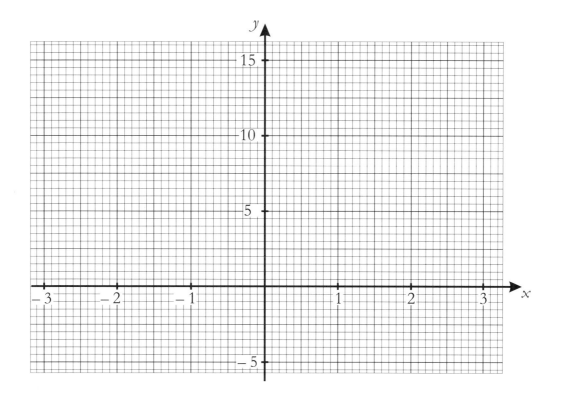

(2 marks)

(c) Solve $x^2 - 2x - 1 = 0$ using your graph.

$x =$ ...., or $x =$ .... *(2 marks)*

Algebra

TRAVEL GRAPHS

A43 Pippa and Sarah took part in a 100 m roller-blading race. Their progress is shown in the graph below.

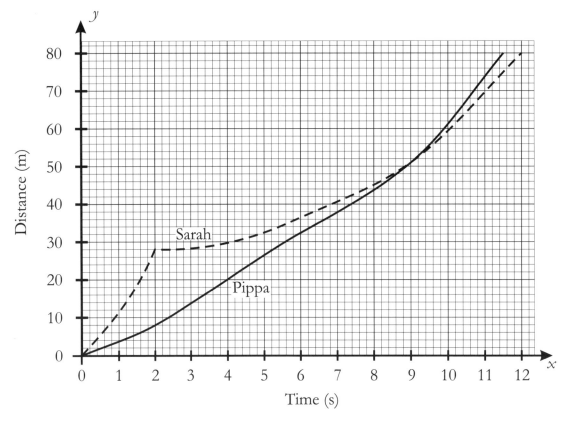

(a) Who won the race?

Answer .... *(1 mark)*

(b) What was the maximum distance between Pippa and Sarah during the race?

Answer .... *(1 mark)*

(c) Who was going the fastest at 9 seconds? Explain.

....

.... *(1 mark)*

A44 Red Rudder and Silver Sails took part in a 10 km yacht race.

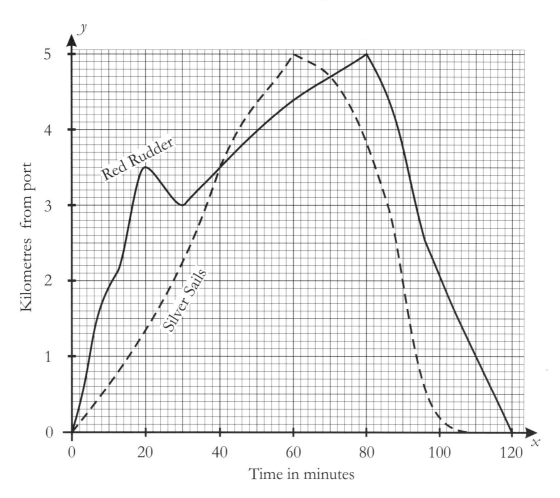

Use the graph above to answer the following questions.

(a) At what time did Silver Sails overtake Red Rudder?

Answer .... minutes *(1 mark)*

(b) Which yacht was in the lead after 80 minutes?

Answer .... *(1 mark)*

(c) Which yacht was travelling fastest as it crossed the finish line?

Answer .... *(1 mark)*

(d) What happened to Red Rudder between 20 and 30 minutes?

.... *(1 mark)*

Algebra

A45 This graph shows the speed of a motorcyclist during a journey.

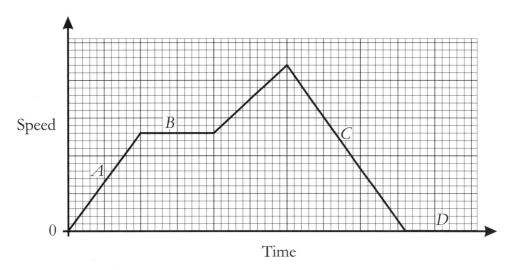

(a) Describe what is happening at *A* and at *C*.

At *A* ....

At *C*.. *(2 marks)*

(b) Describe what is happening at *B* and at *D*.

At *B* ....

At *D*... *(2 marks)*

A46 The graph below shows how the speed of a train varies over its journey between two stations, marked *A* and *B*.

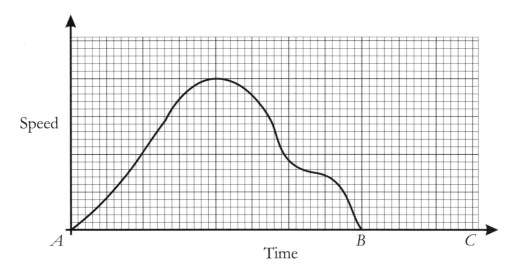

(a) Place a cross on the graph to show where the train was travelling at its maximum speed. *(1 mark)*

There is a third station at C, where the train does not stop. The train accelerates constantly between stations B and C, reaching its maximum speed again at C.

(b) Draw a single line on the graph that shows the trains journey between the stations at B and C.

(1 mark)

A47 Label each graph with its equation.

A: $y = -x^2 + 2$ **B:** $y = \dfrac{1}{x}$ **C:** $y = -x^3$

D: $y = x + 2$ **E:** $y = x^2 - 2$ **F:** $y = x^3$

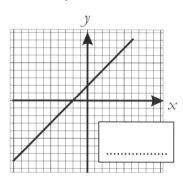 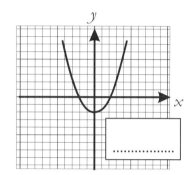 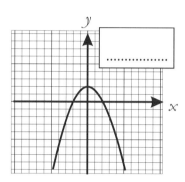

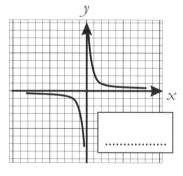 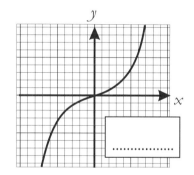 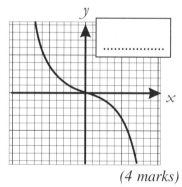

(4 marks)

A48 Which of these graphs cannot be $y = x^2 + 2$? Explain.

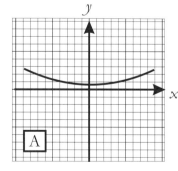 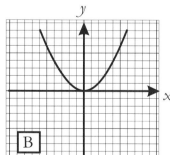 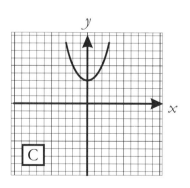

....

....

.... *(2 marks)*

49

Algebra

A49 Water is poured into these odd shaped vases at a constant rate.
Match each vase to the correct graph.

Vase *A* matches graph ....

Vase *B* matches graph ....

Vase *C* matches graph ....

Vase *D* matches graph ....

(3 marks)

A50 Match the following graphs with the statements.

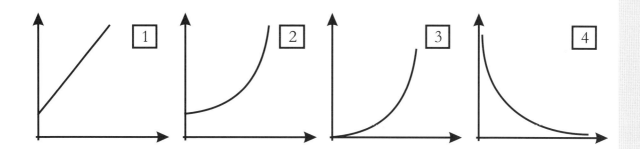

(a) The cost of hiring a taxi per mile including a fixed charge.

Graph ....

(b) $y = \dfrac{1}{x}$

Graph ....

(c) $y = x^3 + 4$

Graph ....

(d) The area of a circle as the radius increases.

Graph ....

(2 marks)

SEQUENCES

A51 (a) Write down the next two terms of this sequence:

1, 3, 6, 10, ..., ...   *(1 mark)*

(b) What are the numbers in this sequence called?

Answer ....*(1 mark)*

Algebra

A52 **(a)** Write down the next two terms of this sequence:

4, 7, 10, ..., ... *(1 mark)*

(b) Find, in terms of n, the nth term of the sequence.

....

Answer ....*(1 mark)*

A53 **(a)** Write down the next two terms of this sequence:

6, 10, 14, ..., ... *(1 mark)*

(b) Find, in terms of n, the nth term of the sequence.

....

Answer ....*(1 mark)*

A54 A sequence of numbers is shown below.

..., 3, 7, 15, 31, ...

(a) What is the rule for finding the next number in the sequence?

....

....*(1 mark)*

(b) What is the missing first number?

Answer ....*(1 mark)*

A55 Below is a sequence of numbers.

..., 2, 8, 32, 128, ...

(a) What is the rule for finding the next number in the sequence?

....*(1 mark)*

(b) What is the missing first number?

Answer ....*(1 mark)*

A56 $1 + (2 \times 3), 2 + (3 \times 4), 3 + (4 \times 5), ...$

The numbers above are the first 3 terms of a sequence.

(a)   What is the next term?

Answer ....*(1 mark)*

(b)   What is the 5th term?

Answer ....*(1 mark)*

(c)   Work out the nth term, simplifying your answer.

....

....

Answer .... *(3 marks)*

A57 $n^2(n-3)^2$ is the nth term of this sequence:

$$4, 4, 0, 16, ...$$

(a)   What is the nth term of the sequence

$$2, 2, 0, 8, ... \ ?$$

Answer ....*(1 mark)*

(b)   What is the nth term of the sequence

$$0, 0, -4, 12, ... \ ?$$

Answer ....*(1 mark)*

A58 Below is a sequence of numbers.

$$6, 9, 14, 21, ...$$

Work out an expression for the nth term of the sequence.

....

....

Answer .... *(2 marks)*

Shape, Space & Measures

S1   Determine the perimeter of this shape:

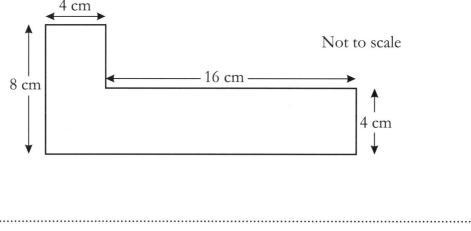

Not to scale

....

....

Answer ....cm *(2 marks)*

S2   Find the perimeter of the shape below.

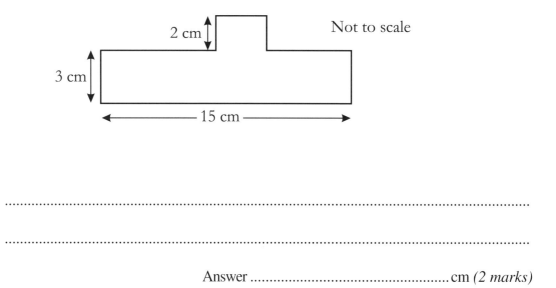

Not to scale

....

....

Answer ....cm *(2 marks)*

S3 A triangular hole is punched out of a rectangular piece of card.

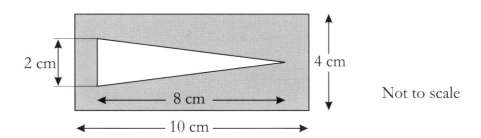

2 cm

4 cm

8 cm

Not to scale

10 cm

(a) Work out the area of the triangular hole.

....

Answer .... cm² *(2 marks)*

(b) Work out the area of the remaining card.

....

....

Answer .... cm² *(2 marks)*

S4

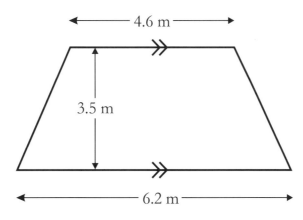

4.6 m

3.5 m

6.2 m

Not to scale

Calculate the area of the trapezium above.
State your units.

....

....

....

Answer .... *(3 marks)*

Shape, Space & Measures

VOLUME & AREA

S5 Below is a solid made from centimetre cubes.

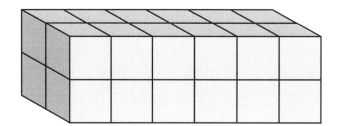

(a) What is the total surface area of the shape?

....

Answer .... cm² *(2 marks)*

(b) What is the volume of the shape?

....

Answer .... cm³ *(2 marks)*

S6

The shape above is made from cubes of side 1 cm.

(a) What is the total surface area of the shape?

....

Answer .... cm² *(2 marks)*

(b) Calculate the volume of the shape.

....

Answer .... cm³ *(2 marks)*

Shape, Space & Measures

S7 **(a)** Calculate the area of the triangle below.

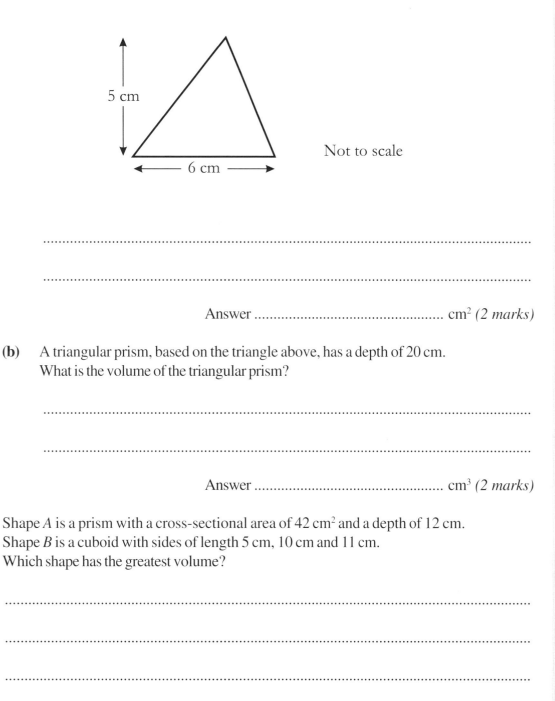

5 cm

6 cm

Not to scale

....

....

Answer .... cm² *(2 marks)*

(b) A triangular prism, based on the triangle above, has a depth of 20 cm.
What is the volume of the triangular prism?

....

....

Answer .... cm³ *(2 marks)*

S8 Shape *A* is a prism with a cross-sectional area of 42 cm² and a depth of 12 cm.
Shape *B* is a cuboid with sides of length 5 cm, 10 cm and 11 cm.
Which shape has the greatest volume?

....

....

....

....

Answer .... *(3 marks)*

Shape, Space & Measures

S9 A triangular-prism shaped box has dimensions as shown below.

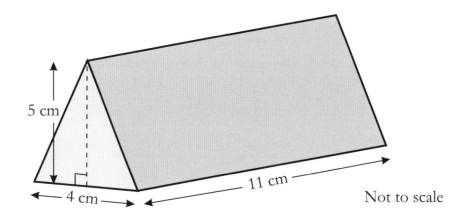

5 cm

4 cm

11 cm

Not to scale

(a) Calculate the volume of the box.

....

....

....

Answer .... cm³ *(3 marks)*

Another box is shown below.

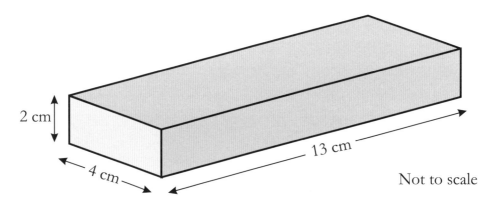

2 cm

4 cm

13 cm

Not to scale

(b) Work out the difference between the volumes of the two boxes.

....

....

....

Answer .... cm³ *(2 marks)*

S10 A cylinder has dimensions as shown below.

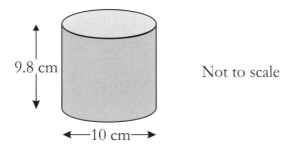

9.8 cm

10 cm

Not to scale

(a) Calculate the surface area of the cylinder.

....

....

....

Answer .... cm^2 *(3 marks)*

(b) Calculate the volume of the cylinder.

....

....

....

Answer .... cm^3 *(3 marks)*

(c) Convert the units of your answer to part **(b)** to mm^3.

....

Answer .... mm^3 *(1 mark)*

Shape, Space & Measures

S11 The drawing shows a cuboid with a triangular prism removed. All measurements are in centimetres.

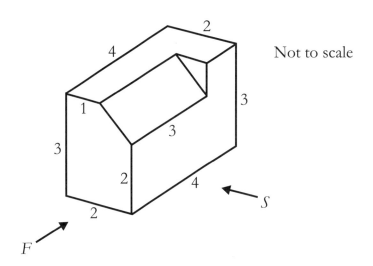

Not to scale

On the grids below, draw full size the front (*F*) and side (*S*) elevations.

Front elevation (*F*):

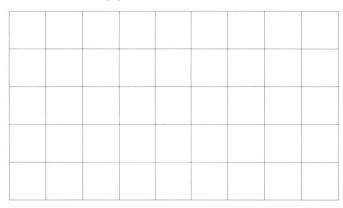

Side elevation (*S*):

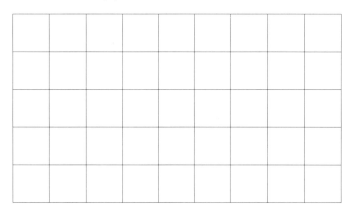

(3 marks)

S12 Two 3-D shapes are combined to form a solid shape.
The plan, front and side elevations of the solid shape are shown below.

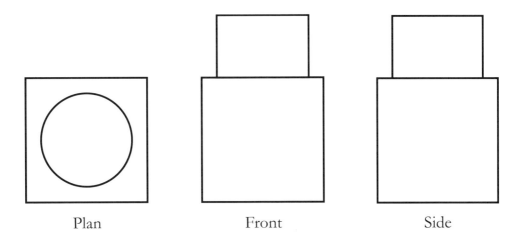

Plan   Front   Side

(a)   Give the mathematical names of the two shapes used.

Answer .... and .... *(2 marks)*

(b)   Sketch the shape.

(2 marks)

Shape, Space & Measures

DIMENSIONS

S13 Steven thinks the formula for the surface area of a certain solid is:

area = $\pi a^2 b$, where a and b are units of length.

Explain why Steven's formula is wrong.

....

.... *(2 marks)*

S14 **(a)** Which of the following formulae could be a volume?

A: $V = \pi r^2 + 4\pi h$
B: $V = r^3 + r^2 h + rh$
C: $V = \pi r^2 h^2$
D: $V = 4rh^2 + r^3$

Answer .... *(1 mark)*

(b) Explain your answer to **(a)**.

....

.... *(2 marks)*

ROUNDING MEASURES

S15 A vet weighed a dog on scales that were accurate to the nearest 10 g.
The display showed the dog's weight as 32.49 kg.

(a) What is the minimum that the dog could have weighed?

....

Answer .... kg *(1 mark)*

(b) What is the upper bound for the dog's weight?

....

Answer .... kg *(1 mark)*

Shape, Space & Measures

S16 A javelin was thrown 52.4 m to the nearest 10 cm.

    (a) What is the minimum distance that the javelin could have been thrown?

    ....

                                 Answer .... m *(1 mark)*

    (b) What is the upper bound for the distance the javelin could have been thrown?

    ....

                                 Answer .... m *(1 mark)*

S17 Given that 1 mile is approximately 1.6 km, which distance is the greatest, 15 miles or 25 km?

    ....

                                 Answer .... *(2 marks)*

S18 Which is the heaviest, 110 lb or 47 kg?
(1 kg is approximately equal to 2.25 lb.)

    ....

                                 Answer .... *(2 marks)*

S19 **(a)** Which metric unit of length would you use to measure the length of a bus?

                                 Answer .... *(1 mark)*

    (b) Using the unit you gave in part **(a)** estimate the length of a bus.

                                   Answer .... *(1 mark)*

    (c) Using a suitable metric unit of weight, estimate the weight a loaf of bread.

                                   Answer .... *(2 marks)*

    (d) Using a suitable imperial unit of weight, estimate the weight of an apple.

                                   Answer .... *(2 marks)*

Shape, Space & Measures

METRIC & IMPERIAL UNITS

(e) Using a suitable metric unit of capacity, estimate the amount of water in a full bucket.

Answer .... *(2 marks)*

(f) Using a suitable imperial unit of capacity, estimate the amount of cola in a full can.

Answer .... *(2 marks)*

ANGLES & PARALLEL LINES

S19 How many degrees are there in:

(a) half a turn?

....

Answer .... degrees *(1 mark)*

(a) $\frac{2}{3}$ of a right angle?

....

Answer .... degrees *(2 marks)*

(b) 0.6 of a right angle?

....

Answer .... degrees *(2 marks)*

S21

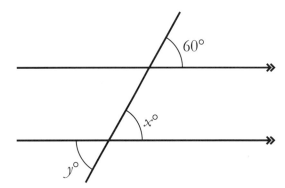

Not to scale

(a) Explain why angle *x* is 60°.

....

.... *(1 mark)*

(b) Write down the size of angle *y*.

Answer .... degrees *(1 mark)*

S22

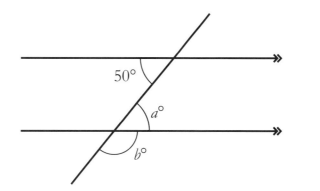

Not to scale

(a) Explain why angle *a* is 50°.

....

....*(1 mark)*

(b) What is the size of angle *b*?

....

Answer .... degrees *(1 mark)*

S23

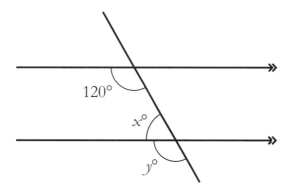

Not to scale

(a) Explain why angle *x* is 60°.

....

....*(1 mark)*

(b) What is the size of angle *y*?

....

Answer .... degrees *(1 mark)*

Shape, Space & Measures

S24

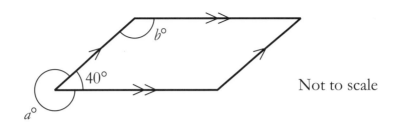

Not to scale

(a) Explain why angle *a* is 320°.

....

.... *(1 mark)*

(b) What is the size of angle *b*?

....

Answer .... degrees *(1 mark)*

CIRCLES

S25 What is the perimeter of the semi-circular shape below?

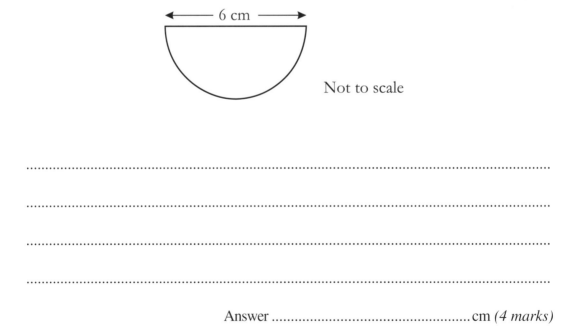

Not to scale

....

....

....

....

Answer .... cm *(4 marks)*

S26

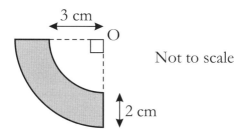

3 cm

O

Not to scale

2 cm

What is the perimeter of the above shape, cut from a circle centred at O?

....

....

....

....

Answer .... cm *(4 marks)*

S27 The turning circle of a radio-controlled car has a circumference of 4 m. What is the narrowest width of road that the radio-controlled car can make a U-turn on?

....

....

....

Answer .... m *(3 marks)*

S28 The circumference of a bicycle wheel is 176 cm.
What is the radius of the wheel?

....

....

....

Answer .... cm *(3 marks)*

Shape, Space & Measures

S29 Find the area of the shaded part of this shape.

3 m

10 m

Not to scale

....

....

....

....

Answer .... m² *(4 marks)*

S30

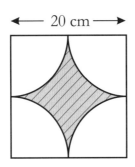

20 cm

Four quarter-circles are intersected with a square to make the above shape.
Find the area of the shaded part of the shape.
Leave your answer in terms of π.

....

....

....

....

Answer .... cm² *(3 marks)*

Shape, Space & Measures

S31 Angle $AOC = 76°$, where O is the centre of the circle.

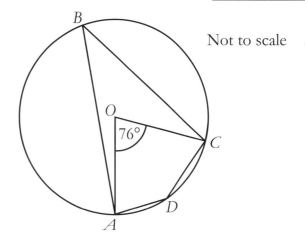

Not to scale

(a) Find the size of angle *ABC*.

....

Answer .... degrees *(2 marks)*

(b) Find the size of angle *ADC*.

....

Answer .... degrees *(2 marks)*

S32 *TA* and *TB* are tangents from *T* to the circle with centre *O*. Angle $ATB = 36°$.

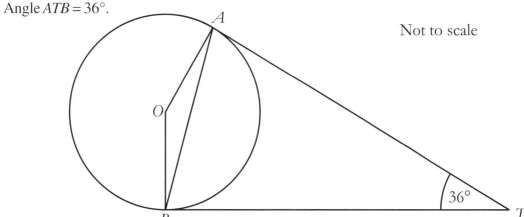

Not to scale

(a) Find the size of angle *BAT*.

....

Answer .... degrees *(2 marks)*

(b) Find the size of angle *OAB*.

....

Answer .... degrees *(2 marks)*

Shape, Space & Measures

S33   *O* is the centre of the circle.
The line segment *AC* passes through *O*.
Angle *ACB* = 38°.

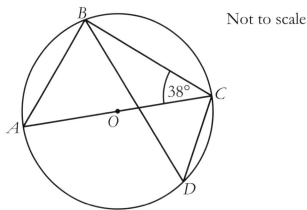

Not to scale

(a)   Find the size of angle *BAC*.

....

Answer .... degrees *(2 marks)*

(b)   Write down the size of angle *BDC*.
Give a reason for your answer.

Answer .... degrees *(1 mark)*

Reason: ....

....*(1 mark)*

S34   *LMNOP* is a regular pentagon.

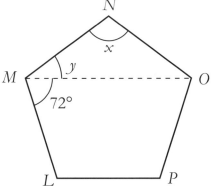

Angle *LMO* = 72°.
Calculate the size of angles *x* and *y*.

Not to scale

....

....

....

....

Answer *x* = ... *y* = ... *(3 marks)*

70

S35 Below is a regular heptagon.
Calculate the size of angle *a*.

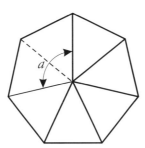

Not to scale

....

....

....

Answer *a* =... *(2 marks)*

S36 (a) Calculate the sum of the interior angles of a hexagon.

....

Answer .... degrees *(2 marks)*

(b) Work out the size of the angles marked *x*.

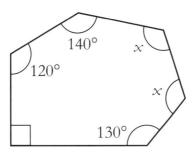

Not to scale

....

Answer *x* =.................................. degrees *(2 marks)*

Shape, Space & Measures

S37

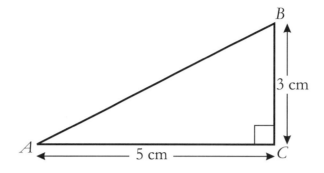

Not to scale

Calculate the length *AB* correct to one decimal place.

....

....

Answer .... cm *(2 marks)*

S38

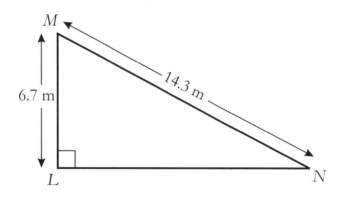

Not to scale

Find the length *LN*.

....

....

Answer .... m *(2 marks)*

S39 **(a)** Use Pythagoras' theorem to find the length *AC*.

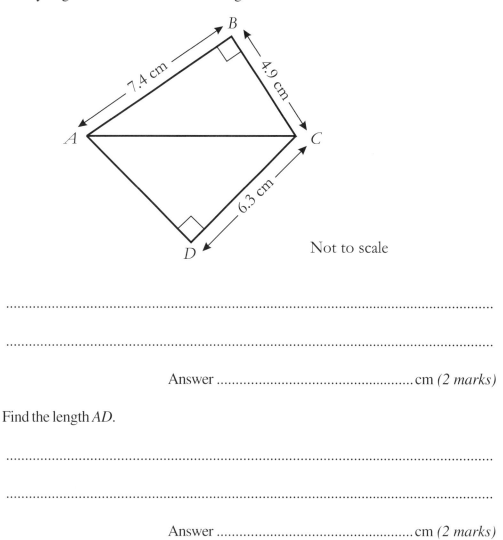

Not to scale

....

....

Answer ....cm *(2 marks)*

(b) Find the length *AD*.

....

....

Answer ....cm *(2 marks)*

S40 A ship sails 14 km due south and then 28 km due west.
By first sketching a rough diagram, calculate how far, as the crow flies, the ship is from its starting point.

Answer .... km *(3 marks)*

Shape, Space & Measures

S41   The line segment AB goes from A (2, 3) to B (5, -1).

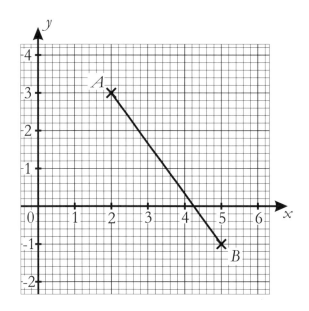

(a)   Work out the coordinates of the mid-point of AB.

....

....

....

Answer (........................., ...) *(3 marks)*

(b)   Work out the length of AB.

....

....

....

Answer .... units *(3 marks)*

Shape, Space & Measures

S42

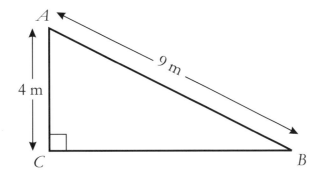

Not to scale

Calculate the angle *ABC*.

....

....

Answer .... degrees *(2 marks)*

S43

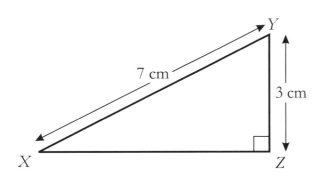

Not to scale

Find the size of angle *XYZ*.

....

....

Answer .... degrees *(2 marks)*

Shape, Space & Measures

S44

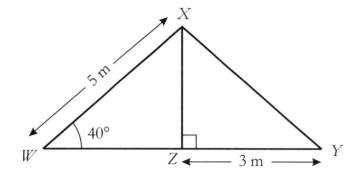

Not to scale

In the diagram above, $WX = 5$ m, $ZY = 3$ m and angle $XWZ = 40°$.

(a) Calculate the length XZ.

....

....

Answer .... m *(3 marks)*

(b) Calculate angle ZXY.

....

....

Answer .... degrees *(3 marks)*

S45

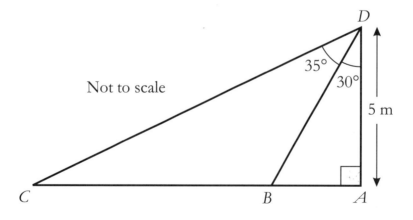

Not to scale

Length $AD = 5$ m, angle $ADB = 30°$ and angle $CDB = 35°$.

(a) Determine the size of angle ACD.

Answer .... degrees *(1 mark)*

(b) Calculate the length *AB*.

....

....

Answer .... m *(2 marks)*

(c) Calculate the length *BC*.

....

....

....

Answer .... m *(3 marks)*

S46 A tree *AB* is 15 m high. Point *C* is 52 m from *B*, the base of the tree, on level ground.

(a) Sketch a rough diagram to show this information.

(2 marks)

(b) What is the angle of elevation of *A* from *C* ?

....

....

Answer .... degrees *(2 marks)*

Shape, Space & Measures

S47 From a point X, Trevor walks 3 km south-west to point Y then 8 km south-east to point Z.

(a) Sketch a rough diagram to show Trevor's route.

(2 marks)

(b) Calculate the angle ZXY.

....

....

Answer .... degrees *(2 marks)*

(c) What is the size of angle XZY?

....

Answer .... degrees *(1 mark)*

(d) Trevor walks back to X from Z in a straight line.
Calculate the distance XZ.

....

....

Answer .... km *(2 marks)*

S48

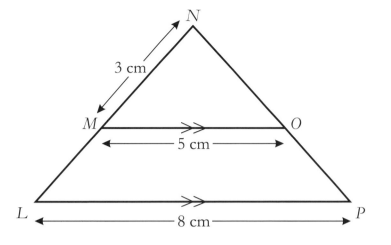

Not to scale

$LP = 8$ cm, $MO = 5$ cm, $MN = 3$ cm and LP is parallel to MO.
Calculate the length LN.

....

....

....

Answer .... cm *(3 marks)*

S49

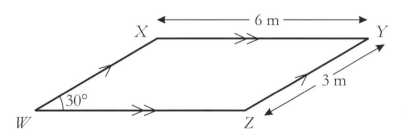

Not to scale

The parallelogram above is enlarged so that XY becomes 9 m.

(a) Calculate the new length of the side ZY.

....

....

Answer .... m *(3 marks)*

(b) What is the size of angle WXY in the enlarged parallelogram?

....

Answer .... degrees *(1 mark)*

Shape, Space & Measures

S50 A design is made up of four congruent shapes, one of which is shown below.
Complete the design, so that the broken lines are lines of symmetry.

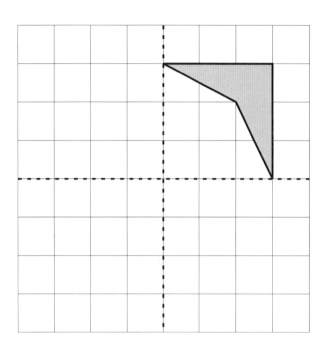

(3 marks)

S51 **(a)** Which of these shapes has 3 lines of symmetry?

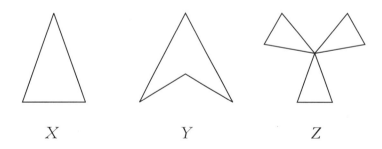

X Y Z

Answer ....*(1 mark)*

(b) Draw another shape with 3 lines of symmetry.
Mark clearly on your drawing all 3 lines.

(2 marks)

(c) What is the order of rotational symmetry of the shape you have just drawn?

Answer ....*(1 mark)*

S52 Below is a map of an island.

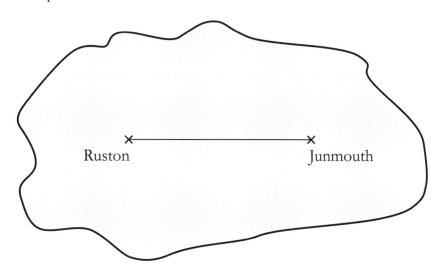

The scale of the map is 1:40 000.

(a) What is the real-life distance between Ruston and Junmouth in kilometres?

....

Answer .... km *(2 marks)*

Marham is on a bearing of 030° from Ruston and a bearing of 300° from Junmouth.

(b) Mark on the map the position of Marham. *(2 marks)*

Shape, Space & Measures

S53 Below is a scale drawing of two boats at sea.
Boat Q is due south of boat P.

×^{P}

×$_Q$

The scale of the drawing is 1:10 000.

(a) How far in real life is boat P from boat Q?

....

Answer .... m *(2 marks)*

(b) Mark on the diagram the position of boat R, which is 1000 m from P on a bearing of 120°.

....

....

.... *(2 marks)*

S54 The diagram shows the positions of three buoys: *A*, *B* and *C*.

(a) What is the bearing of *B* from *A* ?

Answer ....*(1 mark)*

A racing yacht is anchored:

    (i)   along the bisector of angle *ABC*;

    (ii)   along the bisector of angle *ACB*.

(b) By drawing the loci of **(i)** and **(ii)** mark clearly the position of the yacht.

(4 marks)

BEARINGS & LOCI

S55 The diagram shows the position of two electricity pylons *X* and *Y*. David is standing at *Z*.

Scale: 1 cm to 1 km

(a) What is the bearing of *Y* from *X* ?

Answer ....*(1 mark)*

(b) What is the actual distance of *Y* from *Z*?

....

Answer .... km *(2 marks)*

David can see his friend Rupinder at *A*. Rupinder is further north than David.
Rupinder is equidistant from *X* and *Y* and is 5 km from David.

(c) Mark the position of *A* with a cross. *(3 marks)*

S56 The diagram shows the position of three shapes, *L, M* and *N*.

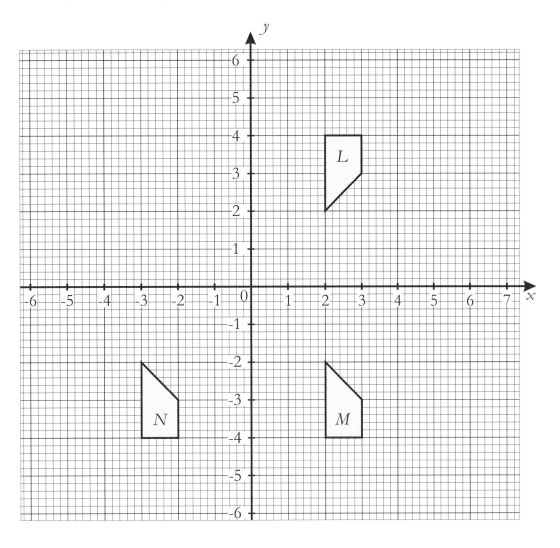

(a) Describe the transformation that moves *L* onto *M*.

....

.... *(2 marks)*

(b) Describe the transformation that moves *M* onto *N*.

....

.... *(2 marks)*

Shape, Space & Measures

S57 The diagram shows the position of two shapes *A* and *B*.

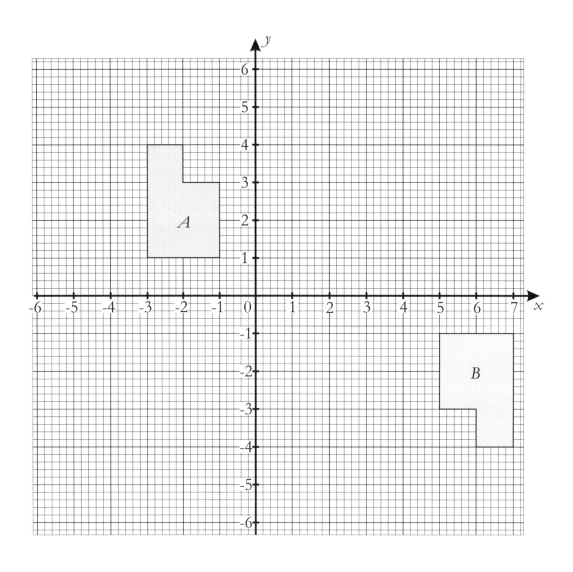

(a) Describe a single transformation that takes *A* onto *B*.

....

.... *(2 marks)*

Shape *A* is reflected in the *x*-axis.

(b) Draw the new position of *A*. Label it *C*. *(1 mark)*

(c) Describe a transformation that takes *C* onto *B*.

....

.... *(2 marks)*

S58

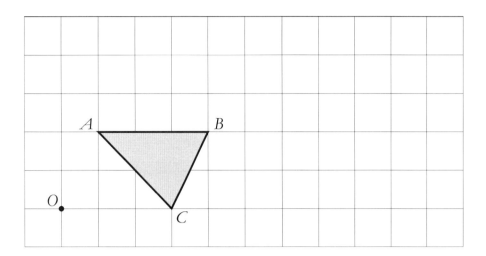

Draw the enlargement of triangle *ABC* with centre *O* and scale factor 2.

(3 marks)

S59

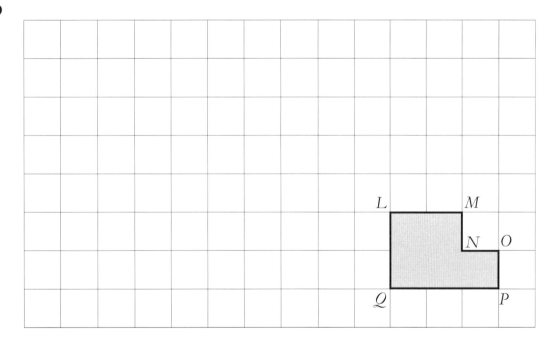

(a) Draw the enlargement of shape *LMNOPQ* with centre *P* and scale factor 3.

(3 marks)

(b) Is the enlarged shape that you have drawn congruent to shape *LMNOPQ*?
Explain your answer.

....

.... *(2 marks)*

Shape, Space & Measures

S60 I once ran the 400 m in 48.6 seconds.
What was my average speed in metres per second?

....

Answer .... m/s *(2 marks)*

S61 A car travelled 182 miles in 3.5 hours.
What was the average speed in miles per hour?

....

Answer .... mph *(2 marks)*

S62 How far would a train, travelling at an average speed of 62 km/h, travel in 90 minutes?

....

....

Answer .... km *(3 marks)*

S63 A man ran at an average speed of 3.2 m/s for 8 minutes.
How many kilometres did he travel?

....

....

Answer .... km *(3 marks)*

S64 A piece of metal has a mass of 5000 kg and a volume of 1.2 m^3.
Calculate the density of the metal.

....

Answer .... kg/m^3 *(2 marks)*

S65 A sample of soil taken from a field has a density of 200 kg/m^3.
25 tonnes of soil is to be removed from the field in order to turn it into a golf course.
What volume of soil will be removed from the field?

....

....

Answer .... m^3 *(2 marks)*

H1 **(a)** Katherine measures the diameters of some beef tomatoes.
The diameters, in millimetres, are:

80, 82, 82, 83, 85, 89, 91, 92, 92, 94

(i) What is the range of the diameters of the beef tomatoes?

....

Answer .... mm *(1 mark)*

(ii) What is the mean diameter of the beef tomatoes?

....

....

Answer .... mm *(3 marks)*

To compare, Katherine measures the diameters of some plum tomatoes.
The range of these diameters is 18 mm and the mean 62 mm.

(b) Comment on the differences between these two varieties.

....

.... *(1 mark)*

H2 **(a)** Younis weighs some English Red apples.
The weights, in grams, are listed below.

55, 56, 56, 57, 59, 60, 62, 63, 63, 64, 65

(i) What is the range of weights for the English Red apples?

....

Answer .... g *(1 mark)*

(ii) What is the mean weight of the English Red apples?

....

....

Answer .... g *(3 marks)*

Handling Data

Younis then weighs some South African Green apples. The range of these weights is 16 g and the mean is 60 g.

(b) Comment on the differences between these two varieties of apples.

....

.... *(1 mark)*

H3 The weights of 9 badminton players are shown below.

75 kg, 81 kg, 74 kg, 84 kg, 74 kg, 78 kg, 83 kg, 74 kg, 83 kg

(a) Find their median weight.

....

Answer .... kg *(2 marks)*

(b) Find the mode of their weights.

Answer .... kg *(1 mark)*

(c) Which of **(a)** and **(b)** is not a good indicator of their average weight? Why?

.... *(1 mark)*

H4 Luke carried out a survey of how much money 8 of his friends had deposited in their savings accounts. The amounts were £47, £55, £63, £57, £82, £4002, £55 and £12.

(a) What was the mean amount deposited?

....

Answer £ .... *(3 marks)*

(b) Find the median.

....

Answer £ .... *(2 marks)*

(c) Look at your answers to **(a)** and **(b)**. Which does not give a good indication of the average savings of the 8 friends? Explain your answer.

....

.... *(1 mark)*

H5 The table shows the number of employees working for a walking boot manufacturer over a three-year period.

	March	June	September	December
1955	68	78	72	42
1956	62	72	75	38
1957	57	64	68	36

(a) Plot the data as a time series on the graph paper.

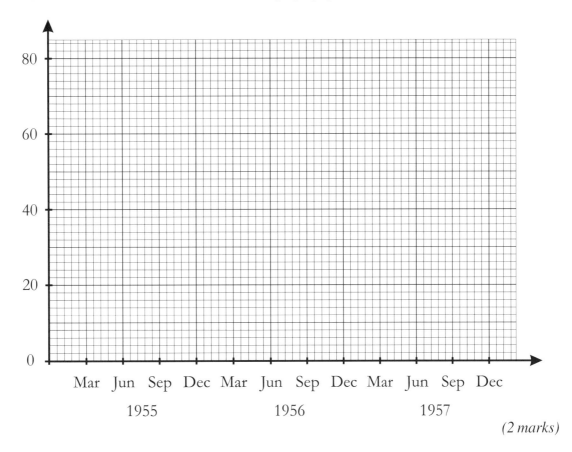

(2 marks)

(b) Calculate the four-point moving average and plot it on the same graph.

....

....*(3 marks)*

(c) Comment on your graph.

....

....*(2 marks)*

Handling Data

H6 The table shows the annual profit (£) of a small shop in a tourist area.

	1st Quarter	2nd Quarter	3rd Quarter	4th Quarter
1998	2100	3400	5800	2700
1999	2500	4700	7900	3200
2000	3400	6200	9700	4700

(a) Plot the data as a time series on the graph paper.

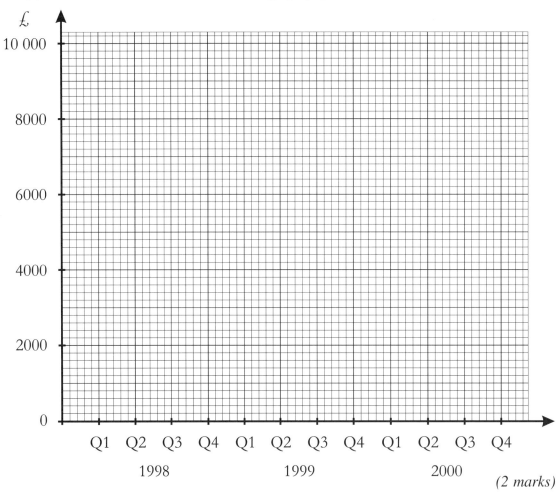

(2 marks)

(b) Calculate the four-point moving average and plot it on the same graph.

....

.... *(3 marks)*

(c) Comment on your graph.

....

.... *(2 marks)*

H7

	Balcony	No Balcony	Totals
Men	18	27	45
Women			47
Children	37		
Totals		101	177

There are 177 people staying at a hotel, 101 of whom are staying in a room with no balcony.

(a) Complete the two-way frequency table above. *(2 marks)*

(b) How many women are staying in rooms with a balcony?

Answer ....*(1 mark)*

H8

	h ⩽ 5 ft	5 ft < h < 6 ft	h ⩾ 6 ft	Totals
Men		8		16
Women	5			16
Totals	8		7	32

The two-way frequency table shows some data on the heights (h) of 32 men and women.

(a) Complete the table. *(2 marks)*

(b) How many of the men are 6 ft or over?

Answer ....*(1 mark)*

Handling Data

H9 The frequency table below shows the number of goals scored by 40 non-league football teams one Saturday afternoon.

Number of Teams	11	13	9	5	2
Number of Goals	0	1	2	3	4

(a) Calculate the mean number of goals scored per team.

....

....

....

Answer .... *(4 marks)*

(b) What is the modal number of goals scored per team?

Answer .... *(1 mark)*

H10 The table below shows the number of eggs laid by 100 different hens.

Number of Hens	Number of Eggs
18	0
32	1
26	2
12	3
8	4
4	5

(a) Calculate the mean number of eggs laid per hen.

....

....

....

Answer .... *(4 marks)*

(b) What is the modal number of eggs laid?

Answer .... *(1 mark)*

(c) What is the median number of eggs laid?

....

Answer .... *(2 marks)*

H11 Toni carried out a survey in her street.
She asked which households kept a dog (D), a cat (C), a bird (B) or no pet (N).
The raw data is shown below.

D C D B N C D N C D N
B C N D D D N C B C N

(a) Complete the frequency table.

Type of Pet	Dog	Cat	Bird	No Pet
Frequency	7			

(2 marks)

(b) Complete the bar chart to illustrate Toni's data. *(3 marks)*

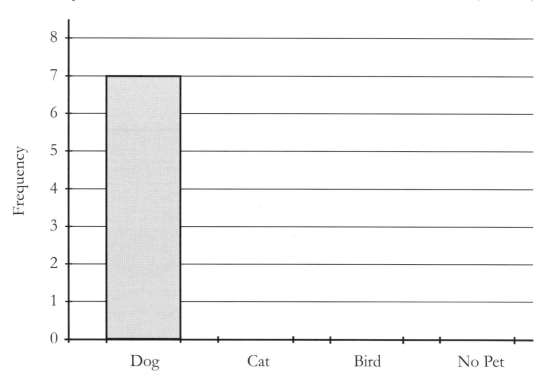

Handling Data

H12 The heights of some flowers are displayed in the table below.

Height (h cm)	Number
$0 < h \leqslant 5$	3
$5 < h \leqslant 10$	7
$10 < h \leqslant 15$	9
$15 < h \leqslant 20$	5
$20 < h \leqslant 25$	4

(a) Write down the modal class.

Answer ....*(1 mark)*

(b) Show these heights in a bar chart.

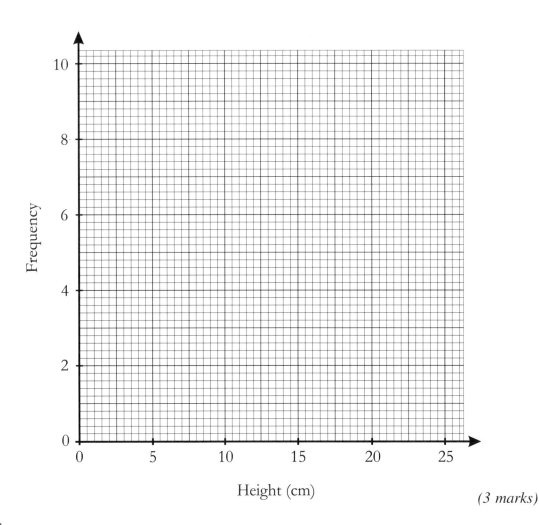

Height (cm)

(3 marks)

H13 Joe carried out a survey to find out how long people spent cleaning their teeth in the morning.

Time (t mins)	Number
$1 < t \leqslant 2$	4
$2 < t \leqslant 3$	15
$3 < t \leqslant 4$	18
$4 < t \leqslant 5$	9
$5 < t \leqslant 6$	3

(a) Write down the modal class.

Answer ....*(1 mark)*

(b) On the grid below, draw a frequency polygon to represent the distribution.

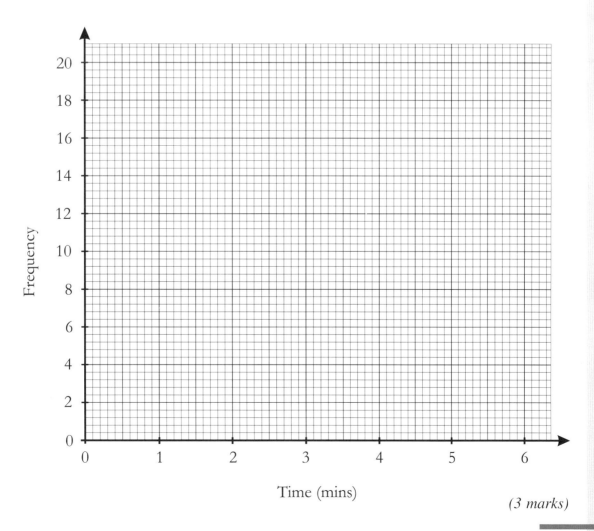

(3 marks)

Handling Data

H14 The deputy manager of a garden centre measured the heights of 25 rose bushes.
The data is given below, in centimetres.

52	54	59	43	41
50	51	52	53	49
47	46	53	49	42
58	56	44	52	48
51	49	47	46	53

(a) Complete the grouped frequency table for the heights of the rose bushes.

Height (h cm)	Tally	Frequency
$40 \leqslant h < 44$		
$44 \leqslant h < 48$		
$48 \leqslant h < 52$		
$52 \leqslant h < 56$		
$56 \leqslant h < 60$		

(3 marks)

(b) Draw a frequency polygon to represent the data. *(3 marks)*

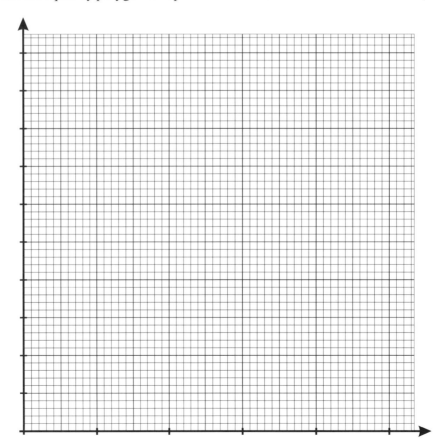

98

H15 Imran timed how long his racing pigeons took to return home after being released some distance away. His data, in minutes, is recorded below.

43	30	50	55	46	37	52	47	41	49
53	44	49	43	50	41	59	45	48	47
47	40	45	58	33	34	42	49	36	43

(a) Complete the grouped frequency table for the times.

Time (T mins)	Tally	Frequency
$30 \leqslant T < 36$		
$36 \leqslant T < 42$		
$42 \leqslant T < 48$		
$48 \leqslant T < 54$		
$54 \leqslant T < 60$		

(3 marks)

(b) Draw a frequency diagram for the times on the graph paper below.

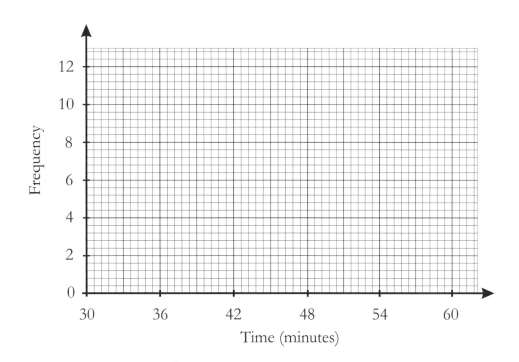

Time (minutes)

(3 marks)

Handling Data

H16 These are the marks obtained by 20 pupils in a science test.

13 42 34 20 24 42 26 29 30 49
33 14 36 38 23 26 42 46 48 31

(a) Complete this stem and leaf diagram for the data.
The first two entries have been done for you.

10	3
20	
30	
40	2

(2 marks)

(b) What is the mode for the data?

Answer .... *(1 mark)*

(c) What is the median?

....

Answer .... *(2 marks)*

H17 Below are the number of shots taken by 24 golfers in the final round of a tournament.

64 87 67 68 95 91 70 83 72 71 73 90
72 64 72 71 65 72 68 81 70 87 69 89

(a) Draw a stem and leaf diagram for the data.

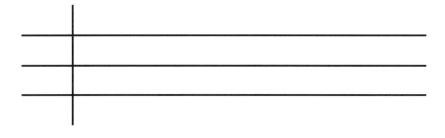

(2 marks)

(b) The median of the scores in the final round is to become the new par for the course.
What is the new par for the course?

....

Answer .... *(2 marks)*

H18 This cumulative frequency curve shows the lengths of time that some people spent in a supermarket.

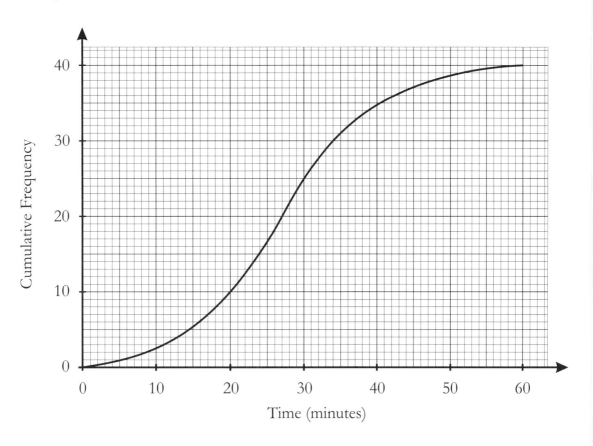

(a) How many people took part in the survey?

Answer .... people *(1 mark)*

(b) Find the median time spent in the supermarket.

Answer .... minutes *(2 marks)*

(c) How many people spent longer than 20 minutes in the supermarket?

....

Answer .... people *(2 marks)*

(d) Find the interquartile range.

....

....

Answer .... minutes *(3 marks)*

Handling Data

H19 Colin is looking for a new front door for his house. He has compiled a table of the prices of 240 front doors as shown.

Price ($£P$)	Number
$500 \leqslant P < 550$	4
$550 \leqslant P < 600$	30
$600 \leqslant P < 650$	50
$650 \leqslant P < 700$	96
$700 \leqslant P < 750$	50
$750 \leqslant P < 800$	10

(a) Use Colin's data to complete the cumulative frequency table below.

$£P$ less than	Number
500	0
550	4
600	
650	
700	
750	
800	

(1 mark)

(b) Use the graph paper provided to draw a cumulative frequency graph of the data.

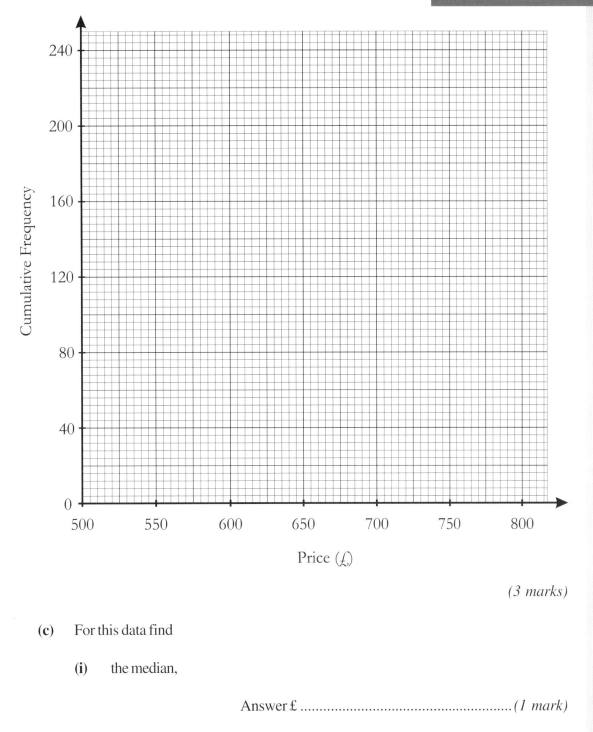

(3 marks)

(c) For this data find

(i) the median,

Answer £ ....*(1 mark)*

(ii) the interquartile range.

....

Answer £ .... *(2 marks)*

Handling Data

H20 The times taken by 160 people to complete an IQ test are shown, in minutes, in the table below.

Time (t mins)	Number
$40 \leqslant t < 50$	8
$50 \leqslant t < 60$	28
$60 \leqslant t < 70$	64
$70 \leqslant t < 80$	40
$80 \leqslant t < 90$	15
$90 \leqslant t < 100$	5

(a) Fill in the cumulative frequency table.

Time (t mins)	Cumulative Frequency
$t < 40$	0
$t < 50$	
$t < 60$	
$t < 70$	
$t < 80$	
$t < 90$	
$t < 100$	

(1 mark)

(b) Draw a cumulative frequency curve for the data, using the graph paper provided.

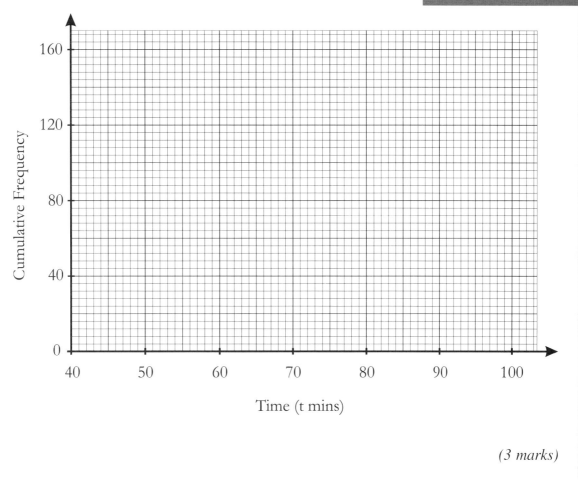

(3 marks)

(c) Estimate the median.

Answer .... minutes *(1 mark)*

(d) Use your graph to estimate the number of people who took longer than 65 minutes.

....

Answer .... people *(2 marks)*

(e) What is the interquartile range?

....

Answer .... minutes *(2 marks)*

Handling Data

H21 Inder drew this box-and-whisker diagram to show the length of time that people spent waiting to log onto the Internet.

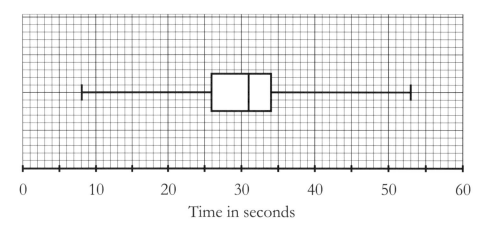

Complete this table.

	Minimum	Maximum	Median	Lower quartile	Upper quartile
Time in seconds					

(2 marks)

H22 The speeds in miles per hour of 11 tennis serves were recorded.
The speeds were:

90, 68, 95, 121, 56, 78, 83, 109, 86, 76, 63

(a) Find the lower and upper quartiles for the data.

....

Lower quartile = ...

Upper quartile = ... *(2 marks)*

(b) Draw a box-and-whisker diagram to show the data.

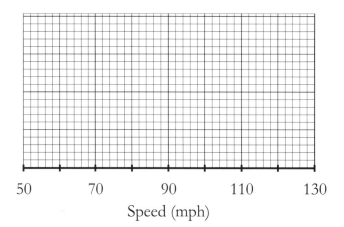

(2 marks)

106

H23 A mobile phone manufacturer makes covers in 5 colours. The pie chart shows the colour distribution of 900 covers sold.

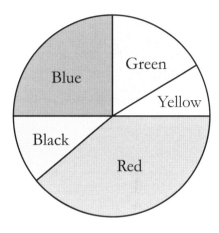

(a) What fraction of the covers sold were yellow?

....

....

Answer .... *(2 marks)*

(b) How many yellow covers were sold?

....

....

Answer .... *(2 marks)*

(c) How many of the covers sold were red?

....

....

....

Answer .... *(3 marks)*

Handling Data

H24 John carried out a survey of 60 pupils in his year at school.
He wanted to know how many CDs they had each bought in the last year.
The frequency table shows his data.

Number of CDs	Frequency	Angle of Sector
0 to 2	12	
3 to 5	32	
6 to 8	11	
9 or more	5	

(a) Construct a pie chart to show this information.

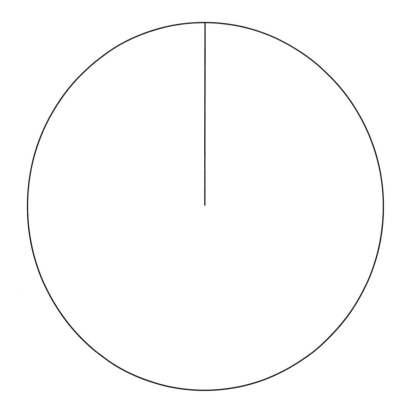

(5 marks)

(b) What fraction of the pupils bought 3, 4 or 5 CDs?

....

....

Answer .... *(2 marks)*

H25 On a certain day last year, an automobile factory produced 180 vans.
The table below shows the colours of the vans.

Colour	White	Red	Blue	Grey	
Number	88	22	18	52	**Total**
Angle					360°

(a) By first completing the table above, construct a pie chart in the circle below.

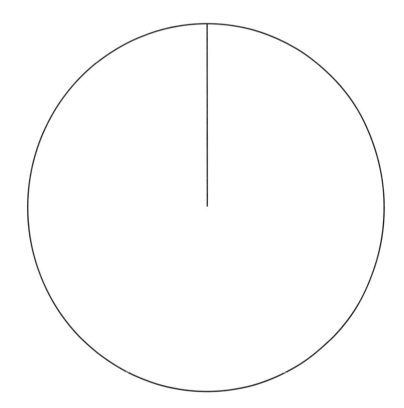

(5 marks)

(b) What fraction of the vans were blue?
Write your fraction in its lowest terms.

....

....

Answer .... *(2 marks)*

Handling Data

H26

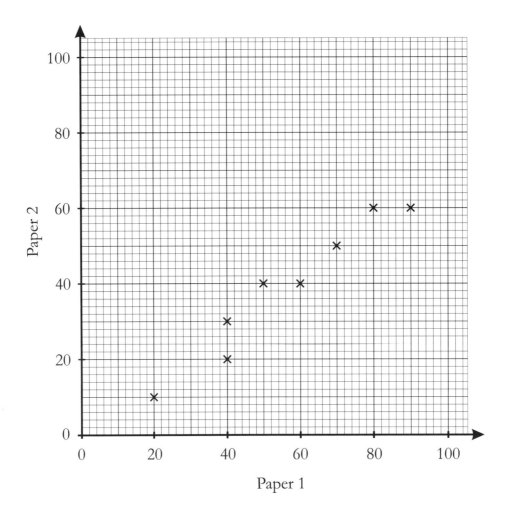

The scatter graph above shows the percentages achieved by 8 apprentices in 2 technical drawing papers.

One student had to miss the second paper, due to illness, having scored 45 on paper 1.

By clearly showing your method on the graph, predict what mark the student would have scored on the second paper.

Answer .... % *(3 marks)*

H27 The table shows the price of 9 cars, together with their top speeds in mph.

Price (£1000s)	12	26	32	15	18	8	22	41	43
Top Speed (mph)	90	114	124	93	101	85	111	131	139

(a) Draw a scatter graph to show this information.

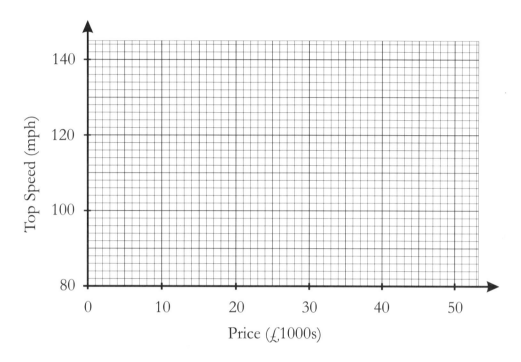

(3 marks)

(b) Describe the correlation between the price of these cars and their top speeds.

....*(1 mark)*

(c) Draw a line of best fit on your scatter graph.   *(2 marks)*

(d) Use your line of best fit to estimate

   (i) the price of a car with a top speed of 120 mph,

Answer £ ....*(1 mark)*

   (ii) the top speed of a car costing £25 000.

Answer .... mph *(1 mark)*

Handling Data

H28

Height (cm)	10	37	31	12	23	22	14	27	16	20
Amount (ml)	23	8	10	22	14	15	21	12	19	16

The table above shows the heights of some fully grown tomato plants and the amount of Thunder Growth Feed given to them each day.

(a) Draw a scatter graph to show this information.

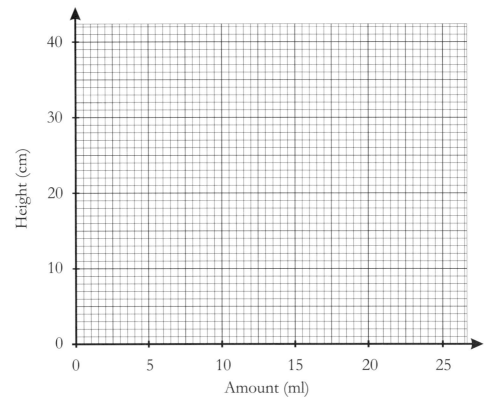

(3 marks)

(b) Draw a line of best fit on your scatter graph. *(2 marks)*

(c) Use your line to estimate the height of a fully grown tomato plant fed 5 ml of Thunder Growth Feed each day.

Answer .... cm *(1 mark)*

The average height of a fully grown tomato plant that hasn't been fed Thunder Growth Feed is 50 cm.

(d) Would you recommend Thunder Growth Feed to tomato growers if they were trying to grow tall plants? Explain.

....

....

....*(1 mark)*

H29 Duncan has carried out some research into how the size of oak leaves varies with their position on the tree.

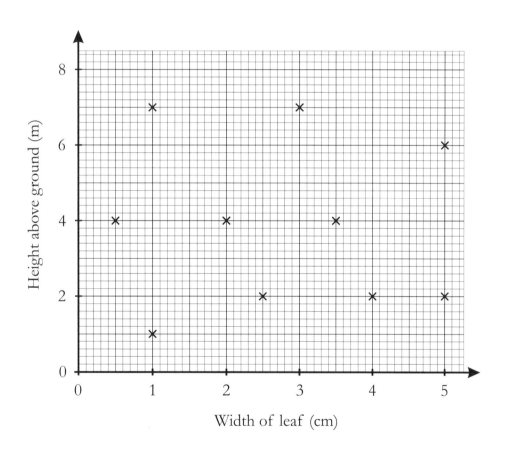

Explain why it is not possible to estimate the width of a leaf found 2 m above ground.

....

....

....*(1 mark)*

Handling Data

H30 The points plotted below show the relationship between the prices of used UltraWheels cars and their mileage.

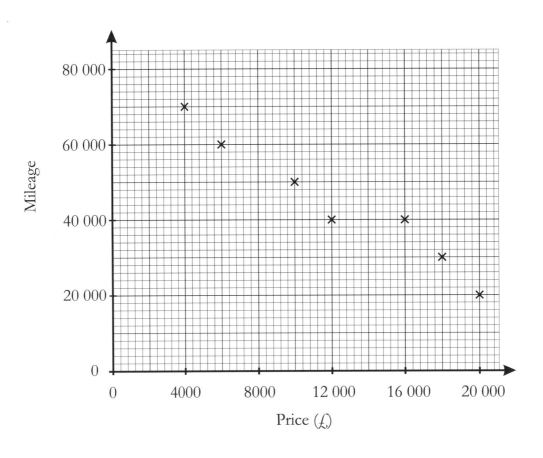

(a) Draw a line of best fit on the scatter graph. *(2 marks)*

(b) Use your line of best fit to estimate the price of a used UltraWheels car with a mileage of 45 000.

Answer ....*(1 mark)*

(c) Describe the relationship between mileage and price for used UltraWheels cars.

....

....

.... *(2 marks)*

H31 A card is drawn at random from an ordinary pack of 52 playing cards.
What is the probability that it is:

(a) a spade?

....

Answer .... *(2 marks)*

(b) not a spade?

....

Answer ....*(1 mark)*

H32 A letter is picked at random from the 26 letters of the English alphabet.

(a) What is the probability that the letter appears in the word CARPET?

....

Answer .... *(2 marks)*

(b) What is the probability that the letter does not appear in the word CARPET?

....

Answer ....*(1 mark)*

H33 An ordinary 6-sided dice is rolled 240 times.

(a) How many times would you expect a 6 to be thrown?

....

....

Answer .... *(2 marks)*

(b) How many odd numbers would you expect to be thrown?

....

....

Answer .... *(2 marks)*

Handling Data

H34 A card was selected at random from an ordinary pack of 52 playing cards. The card was then replaced and another card selected. 520 cards were selected in all.

(a) How many times would you expect a king to be picked?

....

....

Answer .... *(2 marks)*

(b) How many times would you expect a red queen to be picked?

....

....

Answer .... *(2 marks)*

H35 A bag contains red, green and black beads. If a bead is removed from the bag at random, the probability that it is red is 0.2 and the probability that it is green is 0.6.

(a) What is the probability of removing a black bead?

....

....

Answer .... *(2 marks)*

There are 120 beads altogether in the bag.

(b) How many of the beads are green?

....

....

Answer .... *(2 marks)*

Handling Data

H36 In a game, a fair coin is tossed and a fair 6-sided dice rolled.
A head is worth 2 and a tail is worth 3. This score is added to the number on the dice.

(a) Complete the table to show all possible scores.

	+	1	2	3	4	5	6
C O I N	2	3	4	5			
	3	4					

DICE

(1 mark)

(b) What is the probability that the score is

(i) 5?

....

Answer ....*(1 mark)*

(ii) greater than 6?

....

Answer ....*(1 mark)*

(iii) 2?

....

Answer ....*(1 mark)*

(c) If the game were played 180 times, how many times would you expect the score of 3 to come up?

....

....

Answer ....*(2 marks)*

Handling Data

H37 There are three types of cards in an ordinary pack of playing cards: aces, picture cards and number cards.
A card is selected at random, the type of card is recorded and the card is replaced.
A second card is then selected and the type of card is recorded.

(a) Show all the possible outcomes on a tree diagram.

(2 marks)

(b) List all the possible outcomes.

....

....*(1 mark)*

H38 Suna wants to find out how often people use public transport.
He has written two questions to use in a questionnaire.

---

1 What is your name?

2 What type of public transport do you use?

3 How many times a month do you use public transport?

☐ never   ☐ hardly ever   ☐ occasionally   ☐ often

(a)   What is wrong with the first question on the questionnaire?

....

....*(1 mark)*

(b)   What is wrong with Suna's second question?

....

....*(1 mark)*

(c)   What is wrong with the choices offered for the third question?
Explain how the choices could be improved.

....

....

....*(1 mark)*

Answers

NUMBER

N1 (a) £301.32 (b) 27

N2 (a) £527.62 (b) 31

N3 (a) 3, 9, 12 (b) 1, 3, 12 (c) $m = 12, n = 3$

N4 (a) 2, 4, 6, 10 (b) 2, 10 (c) $x = 10, y = 6$

N5 (a) 30 (b) 84

N6 (a) 12 (b) 48

N7 (a) 1 (b) 4

N8 (a) 13 (b) 6

N9 28 m

N10 24 cm

N11 $\frac{1}{4}, \frac{2}{5}, \frac{3}{7}, \frac{2}{3}$

N12 $\frac{1}{2}, \frac{5}{11}, \frac{1}{3}, \frac{2}{7}$

N13 $\frac{24}{360} = \frac{1}{15}$

N14 $\frac{5}{30} = \frac{1}{6}$

N15 (a) $\frac{1}{5}$ (b) $\frac{3}{10}$ (c) 1

N16 (a) $\frac{4}{5}$ (b) $\frac{5}{8}$ (c) $\frac{2}{15}$

N17 $\frac{4}{5}$

N18 £5

N19 (a) $\frac{1}{5}$ (b) 20 (c) 0.002

N20 (a) $\frac{3}{20}$ (b) 15 (c) 0.0015

N21 0.25 cm

N22 0.5 kg

N23 (a) 87.5% (b) 12.5%

N24 (a) 62.5% (b) 37.5%

N25 (a) £15 (b) 61.5%

N26 (a) £35 (b) 36.4%

N27 (a) £23 (b) £28.75

N28 £2.28 per kg

N29 £6.50

N30 £8.80

N31 (a) 120 g (b) 37.5%

N32 (a) 480 g (b) 75%

N33 (a) £10 200 (b) £8670

N34 £5788.13

N35 12.9%

N36 23.8%

N37 (a) £62 609 (b) £71 579

N38 (a) £1091 (b) £1143

N39 (a) 0.002 116 (b) 0.23

N40 (a) 64 (b) 125 (c) 4
(d) 100 000 (e) 81 (f) 64

N41 3.5 m

N42 6.5 cm

N43 (a) 27 (b) 9, 16
(c) 10 (d) $x = 9, y = 27$

N44 (a) 2 (b) 3 (c) 23, 29

N45 $x = 3, y = 13, z = 16$ or $x = 13, y = 3, z = 16$

N46 $a = 19, b = 11, c = 8$ or $a = 11, b = 3, c = 8$

N47 (a) 252 (b) $2 \times 3^2 \times 5$

N48 (a) $5^2 \times 11$ (b) $x = 2, y = 2, z = 1$

N49 (a) 1.14 (b) 1.1

N50 (a) 1.222 (b) 1.22

N51 (a) $\frac{20 \times 50}{500} = 2$

(b) Surface area $\approx 4 \times 3 \times 5^2 = 300$ m^2
There won't be enough paint.

N52 (a) $\frac{400 \times 0.5}{40} = 5$

(b) Surface area $\approx 6 \times 30^2 = 5400$ cm^2
There won't be enough paint.

N53 0.022 to 2 s.f.

N54 0.02 to 1 s.f.

N55 (a) 258 m (b) 86 m

N56 (a) 24°C

(b) Sweden -20°C
France -5°C

N57 (a) -10 (b) -2
(c) -27 (d) -3

N58 (a) 2 (b) 2
(c) 36 (d) 4

N59 (a) 9.2×10^5 (b) 430 000

N60 (a) 4.23×10^{-2} (b) 59 000 000

N61 (a) 8.5×10^8

(b) $(3 \times 10^6) \div (8.5 \times 10^8) = 3.5 \times 10^{-3}$ km^2 (2 s.f.)

N62 (a) 3.84×10^5 km

(b) 110 Moon diameters

N63 (a) $6.2 \times 10^2 \times 7.4 \times 10^{-3} = 4.6$ cm (to 2 s.f.)

(b) $(4.2 \times 10^2) \div (6.2 \times 10^2)$
$= 0.68$ g or 6.8×10^{-1} g (to 2 s.f.)

N64 (a) $(1.8 \times 10^8) \div (1.4 \times 10^7)$
$= 13$ (to 2 s.f.)

(b) $(4.3 \times 10^3) \div (1.3 \times 10^3)$
$= 3.3$ (to 2 s.f.)

A1 (a) $x + 11y$ (b) a^6 (c) $5x^2$

A2 (a) $3x^4$ (b) $\frac{x^2 + 2x}{6}$

A3 (a) $\frac{x^2}{2}$ (b) $2x^2$

A4 (a) $x = \frac{2}{5}$ (b) $x = 4$ (c) $x = 1$
(d) $x = 15$ (e) $x = 12$

A5 (a) $y = \frac{5}{11}$ (b) $y = 2$ (c) $y = 3$
(d) $y = 2$ (e) $y = 12$

A6 (a) $4x + 8 = 32$ (b) £6

A7 (a) $4y + 12 = 852$ (b) 210 g

A8 (a) 15 (b) 32

A9 (a) $\frac{2}{9}$ (b) 11

A10 (a) $T = 20W + 20$ (b) 3 hours

A11 (a) $P = £(6H + 2S)$　　(b) £72

A12 $a = \sqrt{(b - 2)}$

A13 (a) $b = \frac{a}{2c^2}$　　(b) $c = \sqrt{\frac{a}{2b}}$

A14 (a) $a = \frac{v^2 - u^2}{2s}$　　(b) $u = \sqrt{(v^2 - 2as)}$

A15 (a)
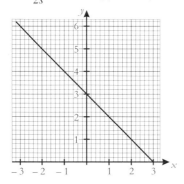

(b) $y = 3$　　(c) -1

A16 (a)

x	0	1	2	3	4	5	6
y	-2	1	4	7	10	13	16

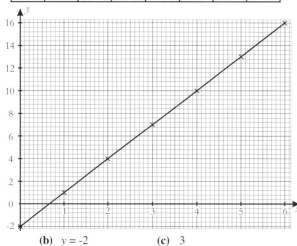

(b) $y = -2$　　(c) 3

A17
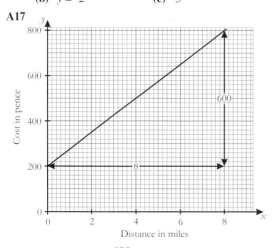

(a) Gradient $= \frac{600}{8} = 75$,

y-intercept = 200,
so $y = 75x + 200$.

(b) $75 \times 10 + 200 = 950$p = £9.50

A18 (a) $y = 10x + 20$　　(b) $10 \times 5 + 20 = £70$

A19 $y = 2x + 18$

A20 $x = -4.5$ and $y = 4$

A21 $x = -2$, $y = 3$

A22
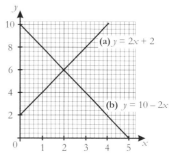

(c) The graphs meet at $x = 2$.

A23
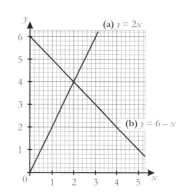

(c) The graphs meet where $y = 4$.

A24 -5, -4, -3, -2, -1, 0, 1, 2, 3

A25 -1, 0, 1, 2, 3, 4, 5, 6

A26 (a)

(b)

A27 (a) $x < \frac{1}{2}$

(b)
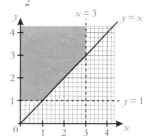

A28 (a) $x < 2\frac{2}{3}$

(b)
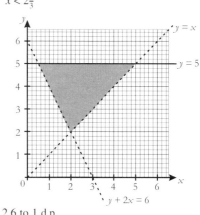

A29 $x = 2.6$ to 1 d.p.

121

Answers

A30 $x = 2.2$ to 1 d.p.

A31 $x = 7.9$ to 1 d.p.

A32 (a) $2x^2 - 5x - 63$

(b) $3x^3 + 3x^2 + 6x$

(c) $(x + 2)(x + 3)$

A33 (a) $15x^2 + 2x - 8$

(b) $2x^3 + 3x^2 + 3x$

(c) $(x + 4)(x - 2)$

A34 (a) $x(x - 4)$ (b) $x = 0$ or $x = 4$

A35 (a) $(x + 3)(x - 3)$ (b) $x = 3$ or $x = -3$

A36 $x^2 - x - 12 = (x - 4)(x + 3) = 0$, so $x = 4$ or -3

A37 $x^2 - 3x - 10 = (x - 5)(x + 2) = 0$, so $x = 5$ or -2

A38 (a) area $MNOP$ = area $ABCD$

$x \times (x + 2) = 1 \times (x + 6)$

$x^2 + 2x = x + 6$

$x^2 + x - 6 = 0$

(b) $MP = 2$ cm (-3 cm is a nonsensical solution)

A39 (a) $16 - x$ cm

(b) length × width = area

$x(16 - x) = 48$

$16x - x^2 = 48$

$x^2 - 16x + 48 = 0$

(c) Possible lengths are 4 cm and 12 cm.

A40 (a) $(x - 8)^2 + (x - 1)^2 = x^2$

giving $x^2 - 18x + 65 = 0$

(b) 13 cm ($x = 5$ gives a nonsensical solution)

A41 (a)

x	0	1	2	3
x^2	0	1	4	9
$y = 3x^2$	0	3	12	27

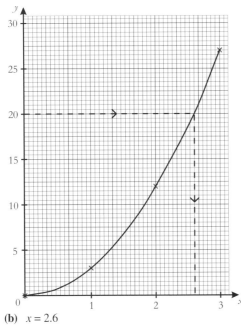

(b) $x = 2.6$

A42 (a)

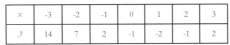

x	-3	-2	-1	0	1	2	3
y	14	7	2	-1	-2	-1	2

(b)

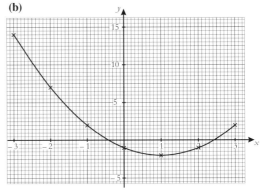

(c) $x = -0.4$ or $x = 2.4$

A43 (a) Pippa

(b) 20 m (after 2 seconds)

(c) Pippa (she overtook Sarah)

A44 (a) After 40 minutes.

(b) Silver Sails

(c) Red Rudder

(d) It headed back towards port.

A45 (a) At A the motorcyclist is constantly accelerating. At C the motorcyclist is constantly decelerating (negative acceleration).

(b) At B the motorcyclist is travelling at constant speed. At D the motorcyclist is stationary.

A46

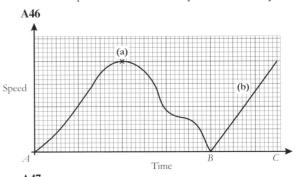

A47

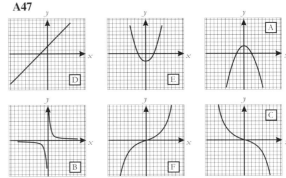

A48 Graph B cannot be $y = x^2 + 2$ because it cuts the y-axis at the origin, not at $y = 2$.

A49 Vase A matches graph 4.

Vase B matches graph 3.

Vase C matches graph 2.

Vase D matches graph 1.

A50 (a) Graph 1   (b) Graph 4

(c) Graph 2   (d) Graph 3

A51 (a) 15, 21   (b) Triangular numbers

A52 (a) 13, 16   (b) $3n + 1$

A53 (a) 18, 22   (b) $4n + 2$

Answers

SHAPE, SPACE & MEASURES

A54 **(a)** Add twice the difference between the previous 2 numbers.

(b) 1

A55 **(a)** Multiply the previous number by 4.

(b) 0.5

A56 **(a)** $4 + (5 \times 6)$ **(b)** $5 + (6 \times 7)$

(c) $n + (n + 1)(n + 2) = n^2 + 4n + 2$

A57 **(a)** $\frac{1}{2}n^2(n - 3)^2$ **(b)** $n^2(n - 3)^2 - 4$

A58 $n^2 + 5$

S1 56 cm

S2 40 cm

S3 **(a)** 8 cm² **(b)** 32 cm²

S2 18.9 m²

S5 **(a)** 56 cm² **(b)** 24 cm³

S6 **(a)** 70 cm² **(b)** 24 cm³

S7 **(a)** 15 cm² **(b)** 300 cm³

S8 Volume A = 504 cm³, Volume B = 550 cm³
Shape B has the greatest volume.

S9 **(a)** 110 cm³ **(b)** 6 cm³

S10 **(a)** $2\pi rh + 2\pi r^2 = 465$ cm²

(b) $\pi r^2 h = 769.7$ cm³

(c) 769 700 mm³

S11

Front elevation (F)	Side elevation (S)
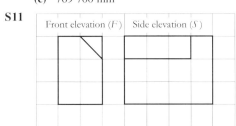	

S12 **(a)** Cylinder and cube **(b)**

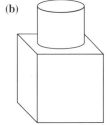

S13 A surface area is always length × length, whereas this formula is length × length × length which is typical of a volume formula.

S14 **(a)** D: $V = 4rh^2 + r^3$

(b) D is the only formula where all the terms are length × length × length.

S15 **(a)** 32.485 kg **(b)** 32.495 kg

S16 **(a)** 52.35 m **(b)** 52.45 m

S17 15 miles = 15 × 1.6 km = 24 km
25 km is greater.

S18 47 kg = 47 × 2.25 lb = 105.75 lb
110 lb is greater.

S19 **(a)** metre **(b)** 12 m **(c)** 800 g

(d) 8 oz **(e)** 9 litres **(f)** 0.5 pint

S20 **(a)** 180° **(b)** 60° **(c)** 54°

S21 **(a)** $x°$ and 60° are corresponding angles and so are equal.

(b) 60°

S22 **(a)** $a°$ and 50° are alternate angles and so are equal.

(b) 130°

S23 **(a)** $x°$ and 120° are supplementary angles and so add up to 180°.

(b) 120°

S24 **(a)** Angles at a point add up 360°, so $a° + 40° = 360°$.

(b) 140°

S25 15.4 cm

S26 16.6 cm

S27 1.3 m

S28 28 cm

S29 23 m²

S30 $(400 - 100\pi)$ cm²

S31 **(a)** 38° **(b)** 142°

S32 **(a)** 72° **(b)** 18°

S33 **(a)** 52°

(b) 52°
Angles subtended at the circumference by the same arc are equal.

S34 $x = 108°$, $y = 36°$

S35 102.9°

S36 **(a)** A hexagon has 6 sides, so the sum of the interior angles is $(6 - 2) \times 180° = 720°$.

(b) $(720° - 90° - 120° - 130° - 140°) \div 2 = 120°$

S37 5.8 cm

S38 12.6 m

S39 **(a)** 8.9 cm **(b)** 6.3 cm

S40

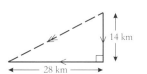

31.3 km (to 1 d.p.)

S41 **(a)** (3.5, 1) **(b)** 5 units

S42 26.4° (using sin)

S43 64.6° (using cos)

S44 **(a)** 3.2 m **(b)** 43°

S45 **(a)** 25° **(b)** 2.9 m **(c)** 7.8 m

S46 **(a)** **(b)** 16°

S47 **(a)**

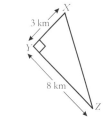

(b) 69.4° **(c)** 20.5° **(d)** 8.5 km

123

Answers

S48 4.8 cm

S49 (a) 4.5 cm   (b) 150°

S50

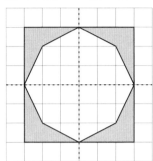

S51 (a) *Z*

(b) For example:

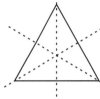

(c) The shape drawn here has rotational symmetry of order 3.

S52 (a) 2 km

(b)

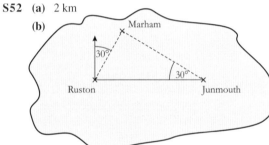

S53 (a) 600 m

(b)

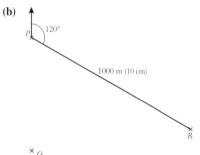

S54 (a) 100°

(b)

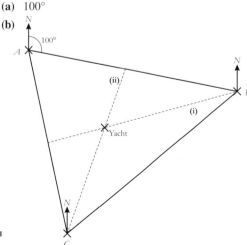

S55 (a) 248°   (b) 13 km

(c)

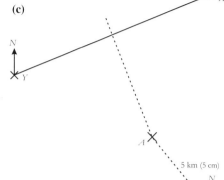

S56 (a) Reflection in the *x*-axis

(b) Translation of 5 units to the left

S57 (a) Rotation of 180° about (2, 0)

(b)

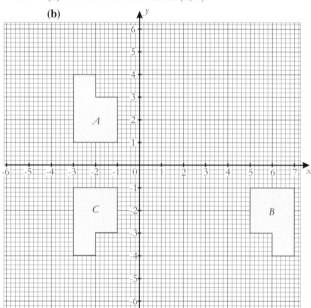

(c) Reflection in the line *x* = 2

S58

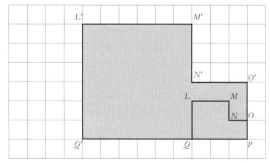

S59 (a)

(b) No, they are the same shape but not the same size. The shapes are similar but not congruent.

S60 400 m ÷ 48.6 s = 8.2 m/s

S61 182 miles ÷ 3.5 h = 52 mph

S62 62 km/h × 1.5 h = 93 km

S63 3.2 m/s × 480 s = 1536 m = 1.5 km

S64 5000 kg ÷ 1.2 m³ = 4167 kg/m³

S65 25 000 kg ÷ 200 kg/m³ = 125 m³

H1 (a) (i) 14 mm   (ii) 87 mm

    (b) The beef tomatoes are generally larger in diameter than the plum tomatoes, and are a more consistent size.

H2 (a) (i) 10 g   (ii) 60 g

    (b) Although the means are the same, the weights of the South African Green apples vary more.

H3 (a) 78 kg   (b) 74 kg

    (c) The mode is not a good indicator. It is the lowest weight.

H4 (a) £546.63   (b) £56

    (c) The mean does not give a good indication, it is distorted by an extreme value (£4002).

H5

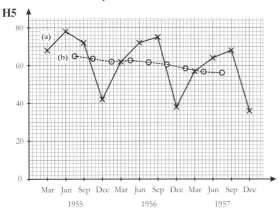

    (b) The four-point moving averages are: 65, 63.5, 62, 62.75, 61.75, 60.5, 58.5, 56.75, 56.25

    (c) The trend is slightly downwards, this could be due to falling sales or perhaps an increase in automation.

H6 (a)

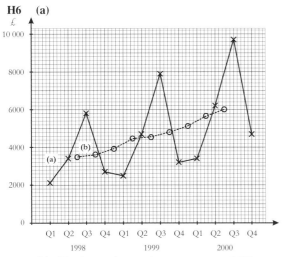

    (b) The four-point moving averages are: 3500, 3600, 3925, 4450, 4575, 4800, 5175, 5625, 6000

    (c) The trend is upwards, this could be due to increasing sales or improved profit margins.

H7 (a)

	Balcony	No Balcony	Totals
Men	18	27	45
Women	21	26	47
Children	37	48	85
Totals	76	101	177

    (b) 21 women

H8 (a)

	h ⩽ 5 ft	5 ft < h < 6 ft	h ⩾ 6 ft	Totals
Men	3	8	5	16
Women	5	9	2	16
Totals	8	17	7	32

    (b) 5

H9 (a) 1.35 goals   (b) 1 goal

H10 (a) 1.72 eggs   (b) 1 egg   (c) 1.5 eggs

H11 (a)

Type of Pet	Dog	Cat	Bird	No Pet
Frequency	7	6	3	6

    (b)

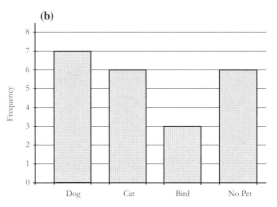

H12 (a) 10 < h ⩽ 15

    (b)

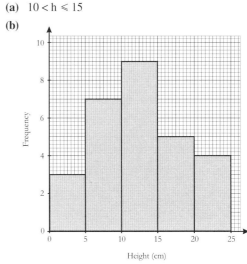

Answers

H13 **(a)** $3 < t \leqslant 4$

(b)

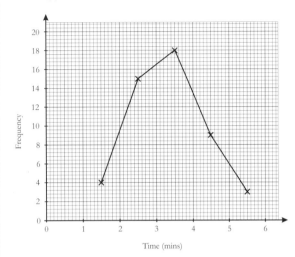

H14 **(a)**

Height (h cm)	Tally	Frequency
$40 \leqslant h < 44$	|||	3
$44 \leqslant h < 48$	⩋	5
$48 \leqslant h < 52$	⩋ ||	7
$52 \leqslant h < 56$	⩋ ||	7
$56 \leqslant h < 60$	|||	3

(b)

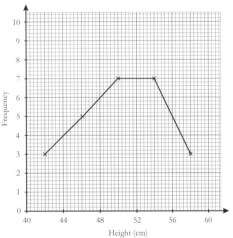

H15 **(a)**

Time (T mins)	Tally	Frequency
$30 \leqslant T < 36$	|||	3
$36 \leqslant T < 42$	⩋	5
$42 \leqslant T < 48$	⩋ ⩋ |	11
$48 \leqslant T < 54$	⩋ |||	8
$54 \leqslant T < 60$	|||	3

(b) This question can be answered by drawing a bar chart or a frequency polygon. Both possible answers are shown on the same diagram below.

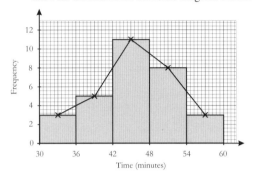

H16 **(a)**

10	3 4
20	0 3 4 6 6 9
30	0 1 3 4 6 8
40	2 2 2 6 8 9

(b) 42   **(c)** 32

H17 **(a)**

60	4 4 5 7 8 8 9
70	0 0 1 1 2 2 2 2 3
80	1 3 7 7 9
90	0 1 5

H18 **(b)** 72

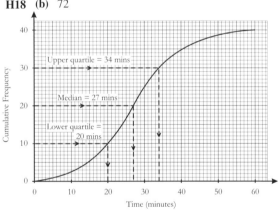

(a) 40 people

(b) 27 minutes

(c) 40 – 10 = 30 people

(d) 34 – 20 = 14 minutes

H19 **(a)**

£P less than	Number
500	0
550	4
600	34
650	84
700	180
750	230
800	240

(b)

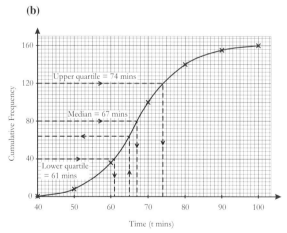

(c) **(i)** £670

(ii) £700 – £630 = £70

H20 **(a)**

Time (t mins)	Cumulative Frequency
t < 40	0
t < 50	8
t < 60	36
t < 70	100
t < 80	140
t < 90	155
t < 100	160

(b)

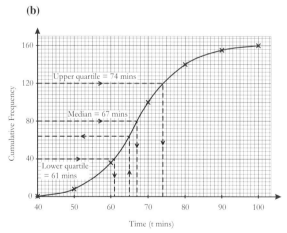

(c) 67 minutes

(d) 96 people

(e) 74 – 61 = 13 minutes

H21

	Time in seconds
Minimum	8
Maximum	53
Median	31
Lower quartile	26
Upper quartile	34

H22 **(a)** Lower quartile = 68, Upper quartile = 95

(b)

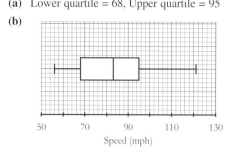

H23 **(a)** $\frac{1}{12}$ **(b)** 75 **(c)** 350

H24 **(a)**

Number of CDs	Angle of Sector
0 to 2	72°
3 to 5	192°
6 to 8	66°
9 or more	30°
	360°

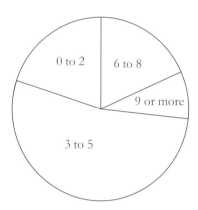

(b) $\frac{8}{15}$

H25 **(a)**

Colour	White	Red	Blue	Grey	
Number	88	22	18	52	Total
Angle	176°	44°	36°	104°	360°

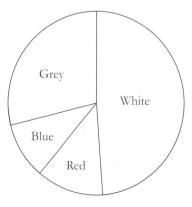

(b) $\frac{1}{10}$

Answers

H26

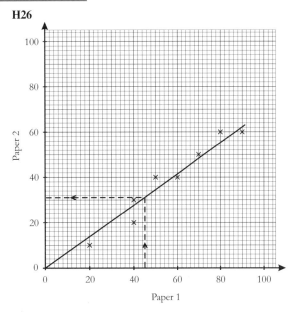

Reading from the graph, the student would have got about 31%.

H27 (a) & (c)

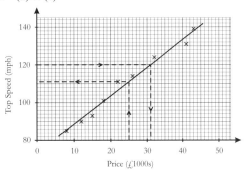

(b) Strong positive correlation

(d) (i) £31 000

(ii) 111 mph

H28 (a) & (b)

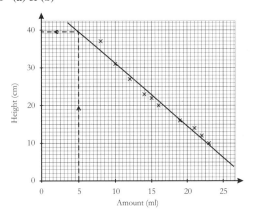

(c) 39.5 cm

(d) No, the more Thunder Growth plants are fed, the shorter they are.

H29 There isn't any correlation between the height above ground and the leaf size.

H30 (a) & (b)

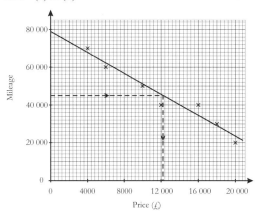

(c) £12 200

(d) Strong negative correlation

H31 (a) $\frac{1}{4}$ (b) $\frac{3}{4}$

H32 (a) $\frac{3}{13}$ (b) $\frac{10}{13}$

H33 (a) 40   (b) 120

H34 (a) 40   (b) 20

H35 (a) 0.2   (b) 72

H36 (a)

		DICE				
+	**1**	**2**	**3**	**4**	**5**	**6**
C **2**	3	4	5	6	7	8
O						
I **3**	4	5	6	7	8	9
N						

(b) (i) $\frac{1}{6}$ (ii) $\frac{5}{12}$ (iii) 0

(c) 15

H37 (a)

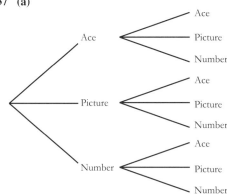

(b) Using A = Ace, P = Picture and N = Number:
AA, AP, AN, PA, PP, PN, NA, NP, NN

H38 (a) People may prefer to remain anonymous.

(a) The question is too vague. Suna should give 3 or 4 choices with tick-boxes.

(b) The choices should be numbers. 'Occasionally', for example, may mean once a month to one person and once a week to another.